PRAISE FOR

BUTCH & SUNDANCE DO INDIA

This is what they would have said if they had read the book--

A rollicking adventure story straight out of the British Raj, told with my kind of humor and irony.

—Rudyard Kipling

Hookah bars, booze and pills, fantastic getaways with harum scarum driving —Gonzo journalism at its best!

—Hunter S. Thompson

India! We shoulda gone to India!

—Robert Redford

I thought about India. The banks are ripe for robbing, but the money ain't worth anything.

—Paul Newman

A great introduction to the 1944-1945 China-Burma-India Theater of War. It made me nostalgic for my camp tent in the Burmese jungle.

—General Joseph W. "Vinegar Joe" Stilwell

No wonder those Americans had culture shock. Imagine ordering a drink with ice!

—Queen Victoria, Empress of India

A wonderful look at Indian culture and history. I remember seeing the giant leech on my visit to India in 1911.

—King George V

Of course we have a god for everything. We need a lot of gods. We have a lot of people.

— Mahatma Gandhi

The road conditions were highly exaggerated. The main highway across Assam will soon have all 793 sections connected to each other. We have very few cattle sleeping in the highway anymore, and elephants are banned from limited access highways altogether.

—Second Assistant to the
Deputy Under-Secretary of
Transportation in Delhi

Excellent coverage of local driving conditions and how to cope with them.

—Wellspring Pharmaceutical
Corp., makers of Bonine

They wasted their time looking for tigers. We made them all disappear.

—Siegfried and Roy

I usually prefer black and white photographs, but the color pix were fabulous!

—Ansel Adams

Also by the author

The Last Romantic War
non-fiction

The Key to the Quarter Pole
fiction

Bush Hogs and Other Swine
Chivalry, Thy Name Is Bubba
humorous essays

BUTCH AND SUNDANCE DO INDIA

A madcap search for our father's WWII footsteps from Delhi to Burma

ROBIN TRAYWICK WILLIAMS

First edition

Author – Robin Traywick Williams
www.robinwilliamsbooks.com

Publisher
Wayne Dementi
Dementi Milestone Publishing, Inc.
Manakin-sabot, VA 23103
www.dementimilestonepublishing.com

Cataloguing -in-publication data for this book is available from The Library of Congress.

ISBN: 979-8-9890973-3-3

Cover design by Jayne Hushen

Graphic design by Dianne Dementi

Printed in U.S.A.

Photo credits: All photographs are from the author's collection except the photos on pages 7 and 137, which were taken by Daniel Novak in his capacity as a U.S. Army photographer covering the war. Map on page iv modified from outline map at MapsofIndia.com.

To Sundance
Thanks, pardner.

INDIA
OUTLINE MAP WITH STATES
& UNION TERRITORIES
TIBET/CHINA
NEPAL
Delhi
Agra
Darjeeling
BHUTAN
Kaziranga
Ledo
Pangsau Pass
Assam
BANGLADESH
BURMA
INDIA
Kolkata
BAY OF BENGAL
International Boundary
State/UT Boundary

PROLOGUE

After two years of reading the likes of "Wrath in Burma," "The Ledo Road," and "The Stilwell Papers," I felt sufficiently educated to decode my father's war stories and write a book about his experience in the China-Burma-India theatre of World War II. But then Dean King said, "You have to go to there."

Go to Burma? Using what connections to keep me out of the Myanmar gulag? I could see myself asking for directions to Shwegu and being lashed to a tree with bamboo slivers jammed under my fingernails.

I was attending the 2007 James River Writers Conference in Richmond. On a narrative nonfiction panel, local—now national—literary star Dean King ("Skeletons on the Zahara") and his colleague James Campbell ("The Ghost Mountain Boys") shared information about the research and writing of their true-life adventure stories. King had trekked around east Africa soaking up the sandy atmosphere where nomadic Muslims ran a cottage industry in the 19th century capturing and ransoming shipwrecked sailors. Campbell had slogged through the steamy jungle-clad mountains of Papua New Guinea, where Americans and Australians fought the Japanese in World War II.

It was axiomatic, they said, that a writer must not only visit but immerse himself in the environment about which he proposed to write. "You have to know what it smells like," they told their audience of nonfiction writers.

I assumed their advice applied to people writing about racetracks or the Hopi Indians, not people like me who were writing about countries with repressive regimes and a history of human rights violations.

I had rationalized my decision to skip this daunting bit of research based on my familiarity with jungle life acquired through the written word. True, the Tarzan books did not have a scratch-

and-sniff feature, but after reading twenty-four volumes, surely I had absorbed some sense of the look and feel of the jungle.

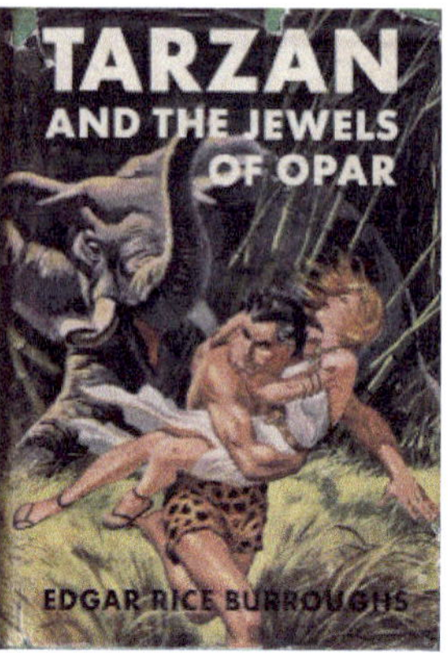

However, Dean, who was doing research for his next book by traveling to China, a country with a repressive regime and a history of human rights violations, insisted that I had to go to Burma. "What's the big deal?"

Faced with the directive from two masters, I developed a longing to go see the Burmese jungle and walk on the Ledo Road. And beyond that, I wanted to see every place my father visited as he traveled around the world in the 1940s: India, Burma, Australia, Egypt, Casablanca and more.

The problem was…there were many problems. Money and personal safety were high on the list, especially for a woman "of a certain age" like me, but those were personal problems. Issues like getting permission from the government of Burma-now-Myanmar and finding guides and transportation in country seemed impossible to resolve without big league connections. After all, I wasn't an established writer with Outside magazine or National Geographic. I didn't think the Goochland Gazette was going to spring for a $40,000 grant to send me to Southeast Asia. Nor did I believe the Gazette had the requisite contacts to help me work out the logistics.

Wistfully I put the idea aside and tried to convince myself there was a workaround via books and movies.

But you never know how your life is going to turn out. Three years later, with a draft of my WWII book in the computer, I found myself planning a family trip Down Under. Our daughter, Katie Bo, had been accepted into an international program related to the Thoroughbred racing industry, and my husband and I were going to visit her in Australia. As I played travel agent to the family, Dean King's words popped out of the back files of my memory: *You have to go there. You have to know what it smells like.*

Eagerly I studied the map. My husband had no interest in going to Burma, but Papua New Guinea is sort of near Australia, and the jungle and terrain there seem virtually identical to that of North Burma, so I tried to work in a side trip. No go. By the time we made our visit to Australia and New Zealand, a side trip to New Guinea would have busted our budget for both time and money. Once again I resigned myself to studying the jungle through books and movies.

Nevertheless, the trip Down Under proved the value of King's advice. My father's ship had stopped in Wellington on the way to India, and it added to the richness of his account for me to see the harbor and see the city where he spent Christmas of 1942. I saw the rhododendron and masses of roses, familiar plants that must have been in bloom when he arrived. I saw the curve of the harbor that gradually revealed the city as his ship sailed in. I saw the few blocks of commercial buildings lining the docks and the Victorian houses stacked up the hillside above the waterfront.

Electrified by seeing what my father saw, being where he walked, I bethought myself of our daughter's educational plans. The following year, Katie Bo would be studying and working in Dubai. Dubai is on the way to India. India, where my father spent most of 1943 training Chinese troops. India, which borders Burma.

Early in 2011, I began planning a trip to India, with side trips to Egypt and Dubai to see Katie Bo and to touch more ground where Dad had passed sixty-six years earlier.

My husband, Cricket, said he hadn't lost anything in India, so I prevailed upon my big brother, Bo Junior, to be my male escort. He is an historian who had helped me with research on Dad's wartime experiences. Recruiting him for a trip to India was something of a feat, since normally Bo will not even leave the Commonwealth of Virginia except to visit family. His last trip overseas was a stint in Vietnam. I appealed to his love of family history and his devotion to chivalric honor, and finally he agreed to go escort his sister and see where his father had spent the war.

Dad spent a year in India—1943—and another year in Burma—1944. But he covered a lot of other ground in his around-the-world travel to and from the war.

For instance, it took Dad fourteen flights and a month to get home from the Burmese jungle in 1945. On one memorable flight, the right engine of the old prop plane caught on fire, and Dad recalled the plane gradually losing altitude crossing Persia (Iran) and the Persian Gulf. Fortunately, by the time they hit the ground, they were in Sharja, Arabia, at an Allied fuel dump. Now a part of the United Arab Emirates, Sharja was then a sand bar covered with 55-gallon drums of fuel as far as the eye could see.

Ordinarily, Sharja would not have rated a visit by traveling historians, but since Katie Bo's internship next door in Dubai had given impetus to the trip, we planned to check "Arabia" off the list.

Dad's next stop after Sharja was Cairo, where he spent several days before hopping across North Africa to Benghazi and Casablanca, so we planned a side trip to Cairo and the pyramids. However, as I was fixing to click the confirmation button, the Arab Spring exploded. We monitored the situation for a week or so, our attention riveted by the flames and rioting crowds, not to mention the death toll. Mom, who was never dissuaded from doing something fun, urged us to go ahead with our plans. "It'll be over by the time you get there." I should mention here the family motto is, *Oh, it'll be all right.*

Nevertheless, Bo and I thought going to India, a democratic nation allied with the U. S., was daring enough, so we scrapped Egypt.

That was about the only travel decision Bo participated in. He refused to be engaged in any of the preparations or discussion of the itinerary. "Do you think we should try to go to Ramgarh?" I would ask. "It looks like the military post has been turned into an industrial area, so maybe there's nothing to see."

Bo would smile and say, "You do the thinking, Butch. That's what you're good at."

So I did the thinking. Of course, this left me open to second-guessing from Bo when things went awry, as they most famously did on March 22, day nine of Butch and Sundance Do India.

ARUNACHAL PRADESH POLICE
WELCOME YOU
CHECK GATE. JAIRAMPUR

Chapter 1

Living on the Edge

The border guard who leaped out of his guard station and flagged down our car carried an intimidating weapon and an angry expression. Waving his rifle in our direction, he spat out a command that even my non-Asamese-speaking brother and I clearly understood.

As a second guard, equally well-armed, exited the weathered building to back up his colleague, Bo hissed at me, "Put your camera away." It was a scene I longed to capture in pixels but, given the anxiety that rippled through the car from our Indian driver and our guide, I thought, *Well, okay, if you insist.*

We sat motionless in the back seat. Our guide, Professor Hitendra Nath Sharma, who was riding shotgun, leaned across the front seat and spoke earnestly to the guard in Assamese with what appeared to be many expressions of innocence.

As we sweated in the back seat, pretending to be invisible, I tried to absorb our surroundings without moving anything but my eyeballs.

Above us curved a faded green wooden arch with the words "Assam Rifles-18th Bn," a memento of the local Indian battalion that had fought the Japanese in Burma in World War II.

All along the dusty road around us were odd structures pieced together out of assorted materials: corrugated tin, bamboo, brick, thatch, teak. Some were dwelling places, some were places of business, sporting old or hand-painted signs. Cattle and the occasional goat browsed the trash-strewn, weedy ground.

Beyond the immediate backdrop, the low end of the Himalayas could be seen sinking to the south, a mere 10,000 feet there. Earlier Professor Sharma had pointed to a notch in the mountains. "Pangsau Pass." *Pangsau Pass*, legendary gateway to North Burma. In 1944, our father drove a jeep down the fresh-cut Ledo Road, crossing Pangsau Pass and plunging into the jungle with Chinese troops to drive the Japanese out of Burma.

The notch was quite possibly just an anonymous ripple in the mountain range, given the Indian penchant for telling visitors what they want to hear. Yet in our quest to retrace Dad's footsteps, we were happy to believe.

Especially since we had been turned back from reaching the Burmese border less than ten miles short of Pangsau Pass. There, a border guard stopped us and listened patiently to Professor Sharma's entreaty to allow us pass. "Let us be going to Nampong. These are Americans. They are wanting to see where their father lived."

No dice. Apparently our father wasn't a big enough name around there to get us through. Sharma shrugged and our driver reversed course.

Then, ironically, as we retraced our own footsteps, we found ourselves in the angry clutches of guards at a gate we had sailed through without even slowing down thirty minutes earlier.

Professor Sharma turned to us. "He is wanting to have your passports."

It's the gulag for sure, I thought as my stomach turned over.

We were 10,000 miles from the United States traveling through a very unsettled tribal region, site of periodic explosions of violence, trying to talk our way across Arunachal Pradesh, a remote state where travel was allowed only by permit from Delhi. A permit, needless to say, that we did not have.

Once called the state of Assam, the region has been broken up into seven smaller states that have seen serious bloodshed over tribal boundaries and loyalties. As we later learned, the upcoming elections had everyone on edge, wary of troublemakers.

The entire former state of Assam is barely connected to India proper by a narrow neck of land. This is owing to the breakaway in 1949 of what is now Bangladesh, a largely Muslim region that split off from India shortly after the colony's independence in 1947.

Here the international boundaries of India, China and Burma are fiercely defended by military representatives of those countries' central governments, even as the many native tribes seek to maintain their own ancient boundaries without regard to national lines drawn in the sand by politicians thousands of miles away. Talk about a cauldron of competing loyalties.

Bo and I smiled thinly and produced the blue booklets proclaiming our U. S. citizenship. Until you hand over your lifeline to American protection to a man with a gun, you have no idea how wild your imagination can get.

In 2009, Iranian guards arrested three young Americans hiking in an area along the Iraq-Iran border. Although they had been warned that the border wasn't, shall we say, clearly marked, they blithely pressed ahead. Of course, the Iranians couldn't pass up the opportunity to pick up a couple of dumb Americans and use them as political pawns. The woman was held in solitary confinement and released in 2010, about six months before our trip. The two men were still in prison as we sweated at the provincial check point. They would not be released until September of 2011. No telling what they suffered.

I thought of them as we sat in the quiet dust of a village in the absolute back of beyond. India is an American ally of course, but if we ran afoul of the locals in this remote area, who knew what might happen? The primitive conditions we endured in spots during our journey across India might seem luxurious in comparison.

How long would it take to bail us out of the local jail? No one back home knew exactly where we were. It would be four or five days before anyone would notice we were missing. Professor Sharma—if he weren't jailed, too—would have no idea whom to contact on our behalf, except possibly the American Embassy (nearest office: Kolkata?). I wasn't even sure he knew our surnames.

"What were you thinking, Butch?" Bo nervously joked.

I was thinking: *This is all Dean King's fault.*

Chapter 2

Dreaming of Ledo

A journey of a thousand miles—10,000, in our case—begins with the first step. The vagaries of airline ticket pricing being what they are, our journey began, not from nearby Richmond International Airport, but from a small airport in Earleysville, Virginia, where we boarded a small plane and flew a small distance to Dulles International Airport. We could have driven to Dulles faster, but we saved hundreds of dollars apiece by taking the puddle-jumper from Earleysville.

In retrospect, that illogical but money-saving first step was indicative of the entire trip, the logistics for which I had arranged by trusting strangers I met on the internet. Originally, when I called travel agencies, it quickly became clear that booking the specialized itinerary we had in mind would be expensive, costing more than a luxury tour of Jaipur, Varanasi and the Taj Mahal. There are places in India that are glamorous, but they were not on our itinerary. What we wanted involved going into the back country, going back in time.

The goal of the trip was to retrace Dad's footsteps in 1943 and 1944, to see where he worked and traveled in India and, with luck, to stand on the Ledo Road where it climbs up to Pangsau Pass and flows down into Burma, to stand there and imagine Dad driving a jeep over the mountain pass into World War II history—a story of romance and adventure that I longed to capture in a book.

The purpose of the Burma Campaign was to provide a lifeline to the free world for Nationalist China, which had been largely overrun and blockaded by the Japanese. Keeping China in the war on the Allied side was a daunting but critical challenge that involved finding a way to provide the Chinese government with supplies, equipment and training to fight the Japanese. Initially, the Allies set up an airlift, flying supplies 500 miles from Assam, India, across the lower end of the Himalayas to Yunnan, China. "Flying the hump" it was called. It was a dangerous mission, flying DC-3s across the steep ribs of 10,000-foot mountains in horrendous weather. Over time, the hundreds of wrecked planes created an aluminum trail below. The airlift was untenable. The Allies needed a road.

General Joseph W. Stilwell, an expert on China and a brilliant military tactician, was assigned to the liberation of Burma so that a supply road could be built from India to China. Stilwell's plan involved building a fighting force out of thousands of untrained Chinese peasants. The British military camp at Ramgarh, India, was expanded for this purpose, and my father, Major H. V. Traywick, asked to be assigned to the project. Dad spent 1943 at Ramgarh instructing troops and then, in 1944, he joined the 66th Regiment of the 22nd Division (Chinese) as a liaison officer for Stilwell as the Allies launched the campaign to drive the Japanese out of North Burma.

The campaign cleared the way for engineers to build the Ledo Road, a +400-mile track from Ledo, India, to Lashio, Burma, where it connected with the Burma Road to China. The proposed route was remote and the terrain consisted of steep mountains, wildly rushing rivers, and jungles filled with tigers, poisonous snakes and Japanese snipers. The whole project—flying supplies in rough weather, clearing the jungle of Japanese, building a road under punishing conditions across brutal terrain—was one of the most extraordinary undertakings of the war.

Dad's war stories created in me an almost mythic image of *Ledo*. Ledo, site of the 20th Evac Hospital where Dad recovered from malaria. Ledo, staging place for the construction of the Ledo Road. Ledo, base for the airlift to China. Ledo, jumping off place for the Burma Campaign. Ledo was Ground Zero. The prospect of actually going to see *Ledo* began to excite me more and more as I worked on our trip plans.

As I wandered around the internet, studying maps of the remote region around Ledo, and making friends with Indians eager to give me advice and contacts, I began cobbling together an itinerary that would get Bo and me out into the farthest reaches of northeast India, into the crushing embrace of the lower Himalayas where China, India, Burma and Bhutan come together in a region of hotly disputed borders.

Assam has been divided into seven new states, among them, Arunachal Pradesh, a state of gorgeous scenery where private entities promote tourism. However, its location in a sweep along the disputed border with Burma and China makes it dangerous and difficult to visit, requiring a permit from Delhi. Political agitators were at the time actively stirring things up and shooting people. Additionally, in a region where as many as fifty-five languages are spoken, the indigenous tribes had—and have—their own ideas about the border.

Nevertheless, ever the optimist, I was determined to drive down whatever remained of the Ledo Road across Arunachal Pradesh and up to the Burmese border at Pangsau Pass. Hopefully, the jungle Dad spoke of so often would be visible from Pangsau Pass.

That was about it for my research goals for this two-week, economy trip.

Dean King probably spends months doping out his research trips: planning to see particular villages, lining up interviews with survivors of The Long March or descendants of the Barbary pirates. Research assistants undoubtedly help him identify obscure museums and cultural shrines, reclusive monks with never-before-seen historical documents.

Other than going down rabbit holes on the internet, I had no way to find the people who knew the people who might know what pieces of the military-industrial complex of the 1940s remained in Assam and where they might be found. So our trip was a bit of a lark, a serendipitous adventure in which we had no preconceived ideas and few expectations other than to try to see India as Dad saw it sixty-seven years earlier.

I plowed ahead blithely making arrangements with people who did not carry the assurances of Viking River Tours or Chase Travel or even Yelp. Most of this was done by email and in internet chat rooms. Occasionally, I made direct contact by phone, which involved negotiating the ten-hour time difference, meaning I got up in the middle of the night to call people in India. Even as I rubbed my eyes and struggled to pin down logistics and prices, I was charmed by the sing-song syntax and liberal use of participles. It was a challenge to understand each other on a connection that often sounded like speaking into a tin can on a string. (When we got to Assam, we saw that tin cans-and-string would have been better.)

Somehow it came together and we trustingly boarded the flight in Earleysville.

We did not know what we would find on the other end, which was exactly why Dean King told me, "You have to go there."

Chapter 3

Bedouins Lost in the Desert

Monday, March 14, 2011

As we flew southeast along the Iraqi-Iranian border, I decided that we were high enough that the Iranians couldn't arrest us like they did those irresponsible young American hikers.

We had flown 6,276 miles in the previous eleven hours, and we had survived pretty well. I was in awe of Bo, who apparently can sleep with his head up as Dad learned to do with the snooze alarm on his ear. My head flops over and I get a major crick in my neck.

When Dad was "travelling for a living" as he called it, selling farm equipment all over the Mid-Atlantic, he often drove a thousand miles a week. By the time he headed home on Friday, he often felt sleepy, hypnotized by the white line. He would report running off the pavement, being awakened by the rumble of tires in the ditch or the noise as he clipped a mailbox. One time Mom bought him a snooze alarm, a device that fitted over his ear and set off a sharp buzz when his head tilted forward on his chest. After Dad tried it one week, Mom asked eagerly, "How did it work?"

"Fine," Dad reported. "It worked just fine. It trained me to sleep with my head up."

We flew the Great Circle route north out of Washington, D. C., up the North American coast past Greenland and Iceland, over Eastern Europe including many countries I've never been to. Can I add them to my life list? We flew east of Bucharest and just west of Kyiv.

At the nine-hour mark, the three of us in our row—Bo and I and a young grad student at Northwestern—all made a pit stop before the rush. Then Bo and I stood around the galley and drank coffee and talked with a stewardess named Diane Brooks. We were flying Emirates and changing planes in Dubai to fly to Delhi. After ten days in India, we would be returning to Dubai. The excuse for making this trip at this time was my daughter Katie Bo's study abroad in Dubai. I planned the itinerary so that we would spend the final few days in Dubai, culminating in attending the Dubai World Cup, at ten million dollars, the world's richest horse race. (Motto: Never miss a chance to go to the races, wherever you are.)

We each had a bag that would pass as carry-on for our four domestic flights in India, plus we had a third bag that held our dress-up clothes for the races in Dubai. India promised to be a rugged trip, so, rather than dragging our dress-up clothes all over India, we put them in one bag that we planned to leave in a locker in the Dubai airport.

We asked the stewardess about the logistics of retrieving our Dubai bag and securing it in a locker for a week. She checked around and reported there were no lockers in the Dubai airport. That seemed absurd because we thought Dubai had the biggest airport in that part of the world. Plus, Kristi with American Express had checked before we left and told us our plan was good. This proved to be the first of many lessons we had in the Middle Eastern custom of locals telling you whatever they think you want to hear. I was already worried about the complications of retrieving the bag, finding the lockers, finding the terminal for our flight to Delhi, and going through whatever additional security they had, so I went into denial about the locker situation. As usual, Sundance was letting me do all the thinking, along with all the worrying.

As folks began to wake up, Bo and I raised the shade and peeked out the window from time to time. I took the first picture on my new camera—the snow-covered Tarus Mountains in southern Turkey. Row after row, as far as you could see.

Then farther on, I could see a river valley feeding into the Tigris. It was sort of amazing to see how close to each other all these places are. This is an ancient land, the cradle of civilization. *Do they teach that phrase in school anymore?* I wondered. Americans traveling through Europe are generally struck with how old the place is. Cathedrals built a thousand years ago and so forth. But the Middle East is even older, and, as Bo and I came to feel, much of the original is still there, under all the dirt and filth.

On the descent, the plane flew straight down the Persian Gulf to a peninsula jutting out of Saudi Arabia into the Straits of Hormuz: the United Arab Emirates, seven tiny sheikhdoms dominated by Dubai. Off to our left we could see a city in Iran, just a tiny spot of light. It was turning night again after a very short day for us. Looking at the Iranian coastline, I was struck by how dark it was. The East Coast of the U. S. this ain't.

As we soon realized, Dulles airport this ain't, also.

It turned out that my confidence in finding a modern, functioning airport in Dubai was grossly out of touch with reality. Although today the Dubai Airport is one of the busiest airports in the world, efficiently handling upwards of 80 million passengers a year, in March of 2011, when Butch and Sundance arrived, the modern complex had been in operation only nine months and was still under construction. The terminal buildings were huge, gleaming cathedrals to air travel, with many sparkling, unmanned counters and wide open marble floors. Unfortunately, the authorities had not yet installed any signage, leaving us adrift in the cavernous complex.

We had packed our Dubai duds in a red suitcase and checked it only as far as Dubai. That meant, even though the stewardess told us there were no lockers, we still had to pick up the red bag and do something with it. To make matters worse, it dawned on us we would have to go through Passport Control *and* Customs, which, based on my previous experiences with international travel, could take a long time. Our layover was three hours.

First we found an information desk and the gal said we could store the bag at Baggage Services.

First problem solved.

Then we waited in an unmoving Passport Control line for awhile. I went to the loo and found a hole in the floor with a spray nozzle on a hose. After some consideration I decided I couldn't handle that with pants and I hopefully tried another stall and found a Western toilet. Good omen.

Then we found an official in a pristine white dishdasha who, when he heard our dilemma, directed us to a special unmarked desk where we got visas and directions to the baggage claim area. The red bag slid past just as we got there.

Then to Customs, where we again outlined our plan. After one false start, the Customs guard just sent us outside to the street entrance for Baggage Services without any pretense of a Customs check. Next problem solved. (At the time, this was an illustrative example of how Dubai worked. The statelet was rushing headlong into the 21st century, building a modern façade on the foundation of an ancient and slowly, very slowly, evolving culture. Despite presenting the image of state-of-the-art modernity, in practice odd aspects of the system were still primitive; the result was dysfunctionality that was alternately amusing and frustrating.)

Finally, we found Baggage Service, a storage room that opened onto the street and was, of course, unmarked. Aside from the fact that customers were wandering around the storage room pawing through luggage without any official supervision, leading me to wonder if we'd ever see our bag again, there was the issue of money. The storage price was forty dirhams/day—about $11. As we were going to be gone ten days, that would be $110. Gulp.

I couldn't bear the prospect of hauling that bag all over India, so we left it with the idea that we would somehow get Katie Bo to pick it up. We left it in her name (naively thinking there was some security involved). Problem solved.

Then we had to find a shuttle and get to Emirates Terminal 3 for our flight to Delhi. It was after 9 p.m. and our flight was at 10:10.

We were a bit harried at that point, fearing we would miss the flight and be stranded in the beautiful Never-Never Land of the Dubai Airport, but once again calmly helpful officials took care of us.

When we got to Terminal 3, we found another enormous palace. It was almost empty and there were none of the usual signs about checking in or departure gates. There was a departure board but it did not have gate numbers.

We had a sense we were just Bedouins lost in the desert as we hiked through this glorious, empty domed terminal, toward the infinitely-receding side where it seemed the airplanes might be parked. Several miles in, we hit a desk where they checked our passports (now with Dubai visa!) and boarding passes. But something was wrong with the boarding pass, so we were directed to another desk, where a nice young woman issued us new boarding passes.

Back to the first guy. Problem solved. (Whatever it was.)

We found the gate just as they were loading, so we had no time to call Katie Bo, because that would have required buying a phone card and we didn't have any Dubai money.

So the last problem was unresolved.

Like the locker issue, I was in denial about losing the red bag. Being in denial became my default attitude throughout the trip. After all, the family motto is, *Oh, it'll be all right.*

However, as our pilot carefully skirted Iranian airspace, it was a reminder that we were in a rough part of the world, where small countries with smoldering resentments and modern weapons live shoulder to shoulder, and being in denial is not always wise.

Chapter 4

Delhi, New and Old

March 15, 2011

When Dad disembarked from the troop ship in Bombay (Mumbai) in January 1943, he was besieged by beggars and shocked by the overwhelming swarm of people. In that regard, nothing had changed in the sixty-eight years since.

By the time we staggered off the plane at the New Delhi airport at 1:30 in the morning, we had been up something like thirty-three hours. Bags in hand, we paused amidst the overwhelming crush of *people people people*. Clever locals pounced on the dopey-eyed tourists, offering us transportation. Somehow we picked one and careened off in the dark to our hotel, which we were conscious enough to notice was protected by a tall wrought iron fence and a locked access gate. Our taxi obtained entrance after relaying our names through an intercom. By the time we fell into bed, it was nearly 4 a.m. Our rigorous itinerary allowed us to sleep only about six hours before we headed out to spend our one allotted day in the nation's capital. Dad didn't spent much time in Delhi either.

The Indian version of LinkedIn is word of mouth. I'm convinced all 1,300 million people in India are networked in such a way that a visitor from, say, America, can find somebody who knows somebody who knows somebody who can fulfill his request. Long before arriving in Delhi, back when I was in Virginia planning our trip, I had made the leap of faith to more or less trust the connections and recommendations of Indian people I met on the internet. I had not shared credit card information widely, but I had developed an itinerary—including airline and hotel reservations—that depended on finding guides and drivers and cars waiting for us at various somewhat out-of-the-way places. (It must also be noted, for their part, the guides and drivers showed up trusting that I would have the agreed-upon amount of rupees in hand.) So I was prepared to accept the word of the desk clerk at the hotel that the freelance driver with a shiny black sedan parked under the *port-cochere* was a reliable chap to deal with. Everybody in India works freelance. Talk about a gig economy.

I'm guessing as a symbol of the emerging middle class in India, our driver Arif probably serves as a good example. To start with, he works as a freelance driver and guide in what they call the hospitality industry. Tourism is an important part of the Indian economy. All of the younger guides/interpreters who helped us had studied for a year or two at "hospitality school". Arif was a little older than the trade school-educated tourism professionals, but he had clearly cultivated the right skills for showing foreign visitors around his fascinating country.

For instance, he had a full-sized sedan that he kept shiny on the outside and clean on the inside. We thought the stock of bottled water for us tourists with delicate intestinal tracts was a nice touch, but in fact Indians everywhere stick to bottled water. Arif had also figured out what clueless tourists like us wanted to see, as evidenced by stops at the Lotus Temple, the Red Fort and the bazaar in Old Delhi. He drove us past India Gate and made sure we met that quintessential Indian character, the snake charmer.

Not only was Arif networked in with snake charmers and rickshaw drivers, he had connections with local guides, shop keepers and restaurateurs. Arif not only took care of us, his customers, he did his best to take care of his contacts in other parts of the Indian economy. While he was taking us to the top tourist stops—the Taj Mahal, Old Delhi—he was also stopping at his cousin's souvenir stand and his brother-in-law's restaurant. Bo and I didn't engage in much shopping, so I hope Arif was not working on commission.

After we struck a deal for Arif to show us around Delhi, he whisked us off through the locked gate out into the smoggy Delhi streets. First stop was the nearby Lotus Temple, a Baha'i house of worship that doubles as a museum. Built in 1986 at a cost of ten million dollars, the flower-shaped white building is surrounded by extensive terraces, pools and flowers. Panels describing the history and theology of Baha'i are mounted along the outside wall of the lower level. As we read them, Bo became fascinated with the unfamiliar faith—a phenomenon that repeated itself over the next ten days. He collected all the fliers and paperwork the faithful made available, while I took photographs of some of the panels for him to study later. Despite being a faith that teaches the value of all religions and the equality of all people, Baha'i followers are persecuted in the Middle East. Imagine that.

India is awash in religions and the people do not spare themselves in their worship practices. For instance, we passed pilgrims who had walked hundreds of miles to collect a bottle of water from the Ganges. In the airport I picked up a book called "Holy Cow," a humorous account of an Australian reporter's year-long attempt to survey and understand all the religions of India in hopes of finding one that suited her. To a certain extent, Bo tried to do the same thing during our ten days in India. Hinduism was probably his favorite, and we were always interested to pick up theological tidbits from our various drivers and guides.

Raised as we were in the Methodist Church, I found Hinduism with its pantheon of gods, including shape-shifters, charmingly reminiscent of Greek mythology. Bo, however, became absolutely entranced with Shiva and Vishnu and Ganesha and a host of minor gods. At one point in Darjeeling as we examined a dark shop with narrow aisles and shelves stacked with metals icons of the holy ones, Bo said, "Hinduism is such a satisfying religion. They have a god for everything." Smug in my Sunday school lessons, I answered, "I already have a god for everything."

Arif drove us around the city a bit—not, I confess to any reader looking for a comprehensive or balanced view of India, through the affluent areas or the modern commercial areas. We went through a business district memorable to me for the sight of

two men and a woman cleaning up rubble out of the street. They had no tools. This was manual labor at its most basic. The woman, dressed in a bright red sari, had a handful of palm leaves—not a broom, just the leaves—with which she swept broken concrete and dust onto a tarp, which the two men lifted and dumped into the back of a stake body truck.

Lorries were not permitted in the city of New Delhi after 7 a.m., although cows had not yet been banned. "Green" buses and other commercial vehicles ran on compressed natural gas. These policies had been instituted in preparation for the Commonwealth Games, held six months earlier, sort of like China's directive to shut down all the factories in Beijing for a month before the 2008 Olympics so the athletes wouldn't pass out from the toxic air. The CNG buses were undoubtedly a good by-product of the Games, but the country was still suffering political problems due to the extreme, even by Indian standards, corruption related to hosting the Games. Plus, the smog was still intense.

Arif drove us around India Gate, an imposing sandstone arch that looks like the Arc de Triomphe. People were walking or picnicking on the surrounding lawn. Known officially as the All-India War Memorial, the monument was built in 1931 to honor soldiers killed in World War I and the Third Indian-Afghan War.

That was about it for Butch and Sundance Do New Delhi. The rest of our brief stay in the nation's capital was spent in Old Delhi, which was fine because that was where Dad went, too, and after all, we were tracing his footsteps.

Arif stopped in a narrow side street and urged us to get out and watch a snake charmer at work. The man squatted on the sidewalk beside a small basket with a lid. As he swayed and played his pipe, a baby cobra slithered out. A second one followed. Sure enough, the two little snakes stood up and swayed to the motion and music. One of them got bored and started to leave, but the charmer snatched him up and put him back in the basket, which sort of undercut the allure of danger he tried to cultivate. The charmer offered to let us hold the snake, but we told him we weren't Holy Rollers.

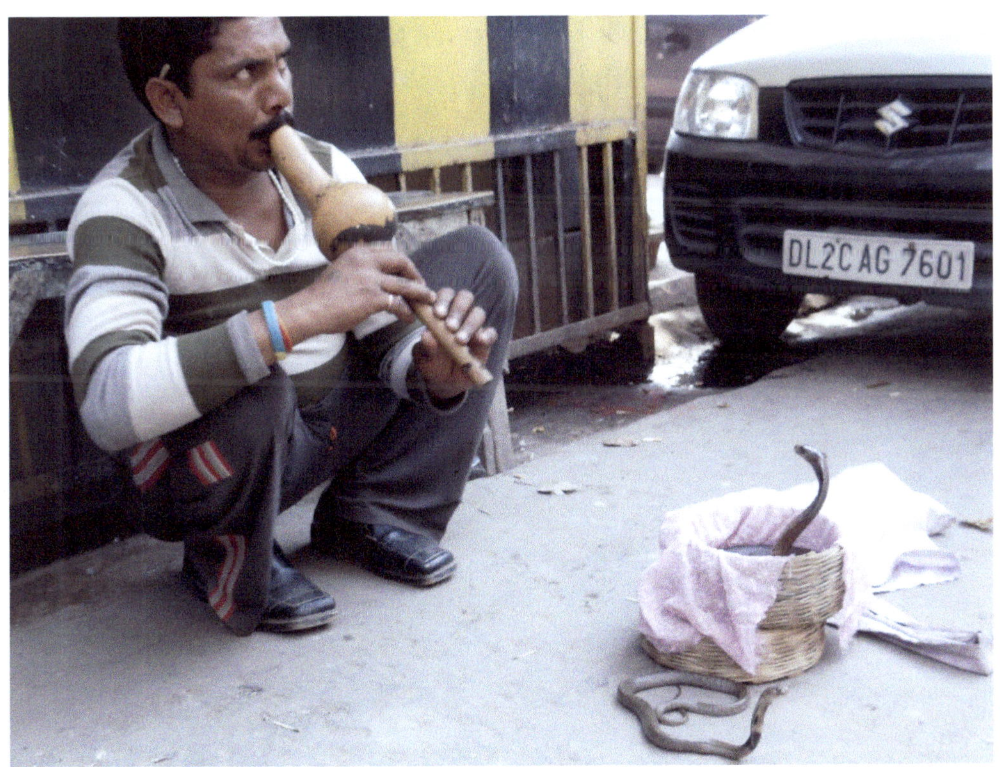

While we were fending off the snake charmer and his petting zoo, Arif engaged a rickshaw to take us to Chandni Chowk, the bazaar in Old Delhi. The streets are narrow and clogged with traffic, he said, and a rickshaw was the way to go. He promised to meet us at the snake charmer's corner in a couple of hours. Given that the streets everywhere are clogged with traffic, I suspect Arif was simply ensuring that we got the full India experience, and indeed, his forethought paid off with our tip at the end of the day.

It was hairy enough negotiating traffic inside a full-sized automobile, but we felt quite exposed in a rickshaw as little toot-toots and motor scooters and bikes and big service trucks all fought with equal vigor for space. Furthermore, our rickshaw man didn't weigh ninety-seven pounds soaking wet, making forward motion a challenge. We were afraid if we leaned back in the seat, we would become a counter weight, lifting him off the ground. We imagined him dangling from the shafts of the vehicle, running in place.

"Maybe we should get out and help him pull," Bo said.

At the bazaar, he threaded his way through shops and shoppers crowded between buildings with balconies and banners hanging over us, blocking out what sunlight could pierce the smog. If you looked closely—which was hard, given the overstimulation of our senses with colors, smells and motion—you could see through the dirt the layers of civilization: a curious column carved in some former age buttressed by a tired-looking former British office of the Raj next to an endless line of nondescript buildings whose architectural history was papered over with signs. Much of the advertising seemed to be for cell phones and internet connections. Amidst the visual confusion, the rickshaw driver proudly pointed to a McDonald's. The place stood out for its familiarity, but did not distinguish itself from the rest of the street by its shine or cleanliness.

Over all, like tinsel on a Charlie Brown Christmas tree, hung a tangled array of electric lines that stretched and looped so low in places they nearly touched the ground.

The odd cow moseyed about but the dominant animal was the dog. Short-haired blond dogs with erect ears trotted through the traffic and nosed among the gutters. Thirty-pound dogs who should have weighed forty, they appeared homeless but not lost. Only one animal that we saw on the entire trip seemed in need of imminent care, a small white hairless dog whose sunburned pink skin oozed fluids.

Our skinny little driver dropped us at a gateway to a park. He pointed through the gateway to a mosque at the end of the street and then turned to point the other direction to the Red Fort. Somehow, he conveyed the notion that he would pick us up in an hour or so.

The street leading to the mosque was broad enough to accommodate vendors squatting on the road cooking on small hibachis and other sellers of scarves and trinkets. There was a field on one side that managed to support a few blades of grass, and we saw a young man leading a roan horse around, much as you would walk a dog on a leash. As we made our way to the mosque, we dribbled rupees and anas to the street urchins, thus acquiring a following of children who begged earnestly but politely. *Baksheesh. Please sahib. One ana.* We could not resist.

We recalled Dad's description of being swarmed by beggars when he landed in Bombay. He was more startled by the breadth of the poverty than the individual beggars. Growing up in the Deep South during the Depression, Dad recalled that there was no money in circulation but no one went hungry; everyone had a garden, a few chickens. But India, which was suffering a famine at the time due to failure of the rice crop, presented a jaw-dropping scene. As Dad recalled, "Back home a fellow might approach me on the street and say, 'Mister Heber, can you loan me a dime?' But India was something altogether different."

Our entourage of urchins trailed off as we climbed a broad staircase to the Jama Masjid mosque, one of the largest mosques in India, with room for 25,000 worshippers. It was built by the Mughal Emperor Shah Jahan in the 17th century. Shah Jahan also

built the Red Fort (or at least one iteration of it) and the Taj Mahal. He was obviously a busy guy.

At the archway leading to the vast open courtyard of the mosque, an official politely informed us that Bo could come in and look around but not I: women were not allowed during worship hours, even if I took my shoes off. Or possibly any time, we weren't clear on that. At any rate, we respectfully stood at the entrance and looked around at the red sandstone and marble edifice for a few minutes before leaving.

Running the gauntlet of children again, we made our way out of the park and crossed the street to the Red Fort. The fort is enormous. An angled red sandstone wall surrounding a vast area, it looked like the Mughals' prototype of the Pentagon, with the addition of a moat. We had the feeling it had not been cleaned since the Mughal era. We paid our rupees and wandered, undirected through cavernous halls to inner areas with occasional signs describing the history of the fort or the current use of certain parts. We found a small museum with artifacts and text relating to the Indian fight for independence from Great Britain, a struggle that began in the 1850s and culminated with formal independence in 1947.

India at that time included what is now Pakistan and Bangladesh. Those two countries were Muslim regions of the predominately Hindu colony. Immediately following independence and after a good deal of bloodletting, those two regions broke away and declared themselves to be a geographically-divided nation consisting of East Pakistan and West Pakistan. The division proved unworkable (Gaza and West Bank residents, take note) and by 1971, West Pakistan had become the Islamic Republic of Pakistan and East Pakistan had become Bangladesh.

Emerging from the fort, we found our rickshaw waiting to deliver us to Arif, who sure enough was waiting at the appointed corner.

We had dinner in the hotel bar with drinks with no ice, in the British way. After some discussion about the risk—what level of purity did the water have that was used to make ice cubes?—we decided to live dangerously and ask for ice. The server graciously brought us one cube apiece.

The other patrons appeared to be Westerners for the most part and we overheard plenty of British accents. The hotel itself had an imperial feel with heavy draperies and furnishings from the Empire, but the bar had a more tropical, rattan look. Delhi itself seemed to have the look of a Caribbean island in places, old colonial buildings weathered by time and hurricanes.

Many patrons were glued to the television screen above the bar, where a cricket match appeared to be in progress. It turned out this was the Cricket World Cup, a round robin affair that would culminate in a few knock-out rounds about the time we headed home. India and Sri Lanka were the hosts. In the spirit of regional congeniality, Pakistan was invited to host some of the matches, but the International Cricket Council cancelled that after an attack on the Sri Lankan team in Lahore.

Getting into the spirit of things, we watched the match keenly, cheering whenever something happened, which we identified by seeing players run around and hearing the announcer's excited tone of voice, because honestly we had no clue what the rules were. It's not even clear how to tell who wins. Runs? Wickets? Overs? Is a wicket a defensive play? Is that how one side prevents the other side from scoring? And who determines how many times a player gets to bat? If he gets a run, does he get to keep batting? Although plenty of data was posted on the crawl, we could tell nothing, but it appeared India won that match, which was a good thing.

The Cricket World Cup followed us around India and we became more and more excited about India's wins—and amused about our own failure to learn what was going on. We cheered animatedly in bars from Delhi to Kolkafa, making profoundly idiotic comments about the play. "What a jolly wicket that was!" "And with only ninety-seven overs remaining!" More gifted writers than I, mostly people who actually know the rules, have written wittier texts about the sport, but no one has had more fun in the moment than Bo and I did.

I was reminded of the time I was on the horse show circuit, a sport that has as much jargon as any other. A beau of mine came to the horse show party one night and stood around through several drinks as the rest of us rehashed the day with impenetrable shop talk. At last, determined to be part of the crowd, my beau summoned all the strange terms he had heard and cheerfully interjected, "What about when that martingale chipped in at the oxer gate?"

I went home to Virginia determined to learn the rules of cricket but gave up. This is a sport so arcane that they play for days at a time to finish one match, probably, I suspect, because they can't remember the score themselves.

Clearly, drinking that one lump of ice burned a lot of brain cells. Or maybe it was lack of sleep.

CHAPTER 5

AGRA AND THE TAJ

March 16, 2011

While Dad was overseas on Uncle Sam's ticket, he could have spent his free time in a bar or a club, blocking battle memories with a bottle, but instead, he took every opportunity to explore local culture and visit famous historical sites, wherever he was. This was a bonus for Bo and me, as it meant we could see the sites ourselves, confident that we were still following in Dad's footsteps.

In May of 1944, Dad was evacuated from deep in the Burmese jungle to the hospital in Ledo with dysentery and malaria. When he was released from the hospital a few weeks later, he was told to take R&R—rest and recuperation. Years later he could still recite the vague travel orders the Army clerk issued him: "Proceed to your destination on temporary duty and upon completion of that duty, return to your proper station."

He hitched an Army flight to the base in Agra, went to see the Taj Mahal, rode a camel out into the Indian desert and then made his way to Delhi.

There he wandered around Old Delhi, mostly noting the layers of dirt on the layers of civilizations built one on top of the other. It did not seem to Bo and me that much had changed in Old Delhi since Dad's visit, and we felt satisfied with our first day of research into Dad's experience of India.

On to Agra.

Pleased with Arif's ability to show us around, we engaged him to drive us to see the Taj Mahal the next day. Agra is about 140 miles from Delhi via dual lane highway. We figured two, two-and-a half hours, but Arif said no, four hours, and even then we must leave early to beat the traffic. We would leave at dawn and stop for breakfast on the way. It seemed strange to think we could average only 35 mph on a dual lane highway, but as usual, we put ourselves in the hands of the locals.

Butch, what were you thinking?

If you take a do-it-yourself tour of India, you will find three issues that are shocking in their extremes but that are accepted as normal by the locals. These issues will impact you in a personal way every day: The widespread poverty, the lack of sanitation, and the dangerous roads. After a semi-genteel introduction to the former British colony on day one, we now faced India—and Indian traffic—head-on.

As we came to learn all too well, 35 mph is a generous average when figuring the driving time between two places in India. Basically, you look at the map, estimate the time it would take if you were in America, and double or triple it.

That's because in India at that time there was no such thing as a limited access highway. In those days before the Yamuna Expressway, we found the divided highway from Delhi to Agra to be a good road, two lanes each way, in good repair, with a median exploding with mounds of magenta bougainvillea. But the road was chock-a-block with vehicles of all sizes and speeds, including sedans like ours and big lorries, as well as motorized auto-rickshaws that top out at 25-30 mph and mini cars and motor scooters loaded down with sometimes four people. In addition, there were hay wagons hitched to camels, bicycles, pedestrians carrying bundles of sticks, and women in saris with bowls of cow dung on their heads. In our more rural travels, we passed boys riding elephants on the road. And everywhere, walking, sleeping, rooting in trash, walking some more, always seemingly in a world far removed from the cacophony and potential mayhem around them were cows. Cows. Bullocks. Calves. Really baby calves. All wearing an absolutely blank expression. Sacred, untouchable cows. (Even more untouchable now under the administration of PM Modi, who has promoted sacred-cow-Hinduism to the detriment of beef-eating, anti-pork Muslims.)

When Bo and I were planning our trip, we were told in no uncertain terms not to even think about renting a car and driving ourselves. It takes guts and plenty of medication just to be a passenger in a car in India. I'm unfortunately prone to motion-sickness, and I ingested more Bonine than food while we were there.

Much of the road to Agra was divided by a median but most highways are not. There are no lanes, as such, despite occasional markings, but the center pathway is reserved by custom for the fastest vehicles, with paths for slower modes of travel fanning out towards the shoulder. The center "lane" is also two-way. With so many elements trying to occupy the same space at the same time, as they do a thousand times a day on each mile of road, then someone has to give way, and occasionally, even if you are in an SUV, this may be you.

Thus, when our hired car, traveling 50 mph, met a Tata truck coming the other way in the center lane, the vehicles had to dodge each other. This is accomplished without using brakes. The two vehicles bear down on each other at a closing speed of 100 mph, hemmed in on both sides by rickshaws, camels and motorbikes, and at the last second, each driver jerks his wheel to the left. The slower vehicles all lean to the left just enough to allow the faster vehicles to pass each other, and then everyone moves back towards the middle. It is a beautifully coordinated maneuver, executed millions of times a day, but no foreigner could ever learn it. Indian drivers have nerves of steel and a confident grasp of the exact width of their vehicles. I can't imagine how they test for that with the driver's license exam.

People over sixty might remember a similar arrangement in 1950s America, the death-trap three-lane highway with the center lane reserved for passing—both directions. American drivers thus mimicked Indian drivers for a brief span until American highway engineers, noting the high incidence of head-on collisions, introduced dual-lane divided roads.

Arif told us he would stop at a nice place for breakfast about thirty minutes out. However, the sun had forced its way through the smog and we had driven many terrifying miles before the idea of breakfast came up. Honestly, we were so gob-smacked we might never have thought of food again if he hadn't stopped.

When we could tear our eyes away from on-rushing death on the highway, this is what we saw:

To start with, even out in the country, it was still very smoggy. The countryside was flat with few trees and large uncultivated areas of weeds and bare earth. Amidst the open land there were odd rectangular brick walls, enclosing maybe half an acre, with nothing inside except some trash or rubble. We learned the walls were delineating a piece of private property. This area had the occasional hotel with a low wall and a spot of landscaping. With no nearby amenities or attractions, the hotels seemed to be random installations in the barren landscape. Although we did not pass land under cultivation, Arif spoke of farmers growing wheat and raising mustard for the seeds. Currently it was the height of the potato harvest. In the villages and on the road we saw many farm wagons and tractors. We saw camels hauling wagons of hay wrapped in burlap like a bale of cotton. Hay is also stored in a large sheaf that looks like a grass hut with a pointed roof—to shed the rain, we guessed.

A brightly painted blue-and-gold statue of Shiva fifty feet high stood guard over a trash lot by the side of the road. July is the month of Shiva, when thousands of people go to the Ganges and get holy water. It's 250 km (155 miles) from here. They walk. Even though it was March, we saw them walking home with "cowers"—tinsel-covered, bow-shaped rigs with containers of holy water, which they take home and pour on Shiva in the temple.

Arif gave us an overview of the Hindu gods, thus continuing Bo's religious education.

Ganesha – This one has the head of an elephant. Pray to this one first, before any important undertaking, then pray to other gods.

Shiva – This one is white with a blue neck and is often shown with four arms. Known as "the destroyer," the god of destruction and rebirth.

Brahma – Known as the "generator" or "creator."

Vishnu – This one is powerful. Known as the "operator."

Cattle are so plentiful it hardly bears mentioning. They breed the cows to get them to freshen for the milk and if the resulting calf is a bull calf, they leave him loose, so the bullocks grow up unrestrained and apparently of uncertain ownership. (It's possible that Arif the city boy did not know what he was talking about because later we learned that bullocks are highly prized and used to plow. And although cattle roam freely everywhere, children are dispatched in the evening to round them up and bring them home.) A cow is often chained up and fed at home. Several times we saw a cow chained so short she couldn't raise her head.

Cattle aren't the only livestock roaming loose. We saw other animals nosing about individually or in small groups: Pigs, goats, chickens, dogs, sheep. Ownership is a serious matter in a place where poverty is widespread, but somehow the people figure it out, even without pens and fences.

There were people urinating everywhere. This vision cannot be overstated. Men and women respond to the call of nature along the side of the road, next to buildings, under trees, beside walls or simply out in the open. Dad recalled being shocked equally by the immodesty and the unsanitary aspect of this behavior. (Three years after our visit, Prime Minister Narendra Modi announced a five-year plan to end public defecation. By 2019, more than 100 million toilets had been built, and India was declared ODF—open-defecation free—a declaration that was widely disputed.) Personally, after seeing some of the "bathrooms" at rural restaurants, I became a little more understanding of going *en pleine aire*. Meanwhile, we saw this sign: "Spitting is prohibited here."

Contradictions abound in India and are part of the country's charm.

There were mixed signs of industry and commercial growth amid all the poverty. We saw a lot of buildings under construction but no one actually working on them. In one typical case, we passed a half-built building with prickly shafts of re-bar sticking out the top of the unfinished brick walls next to a tent city with a herd of cattle and a hog.

The roads seethed with energy. Tractors and combines on their way to the harvest added to the traffic congestion. Commercial vehicles of all sizes plied the road in both directions. At one point we saw a mule hitched to a flat-bed wagon trotting briskly and purposefully along the shoulder of the road, all alone. Vehicles frequently drove the wrong way on the shoulder. All morning on the way to Agra we saw people making their way, often on foot, somewhere to scavenge a living. In the evening on the way back to Delhi, we saw men carrying bundles of sticks or sacks of potatoes or women balancing big bowls of cow dung on their heads. The dung is dried into patties and burned for fuel. The smoking patties also keep mosquitoes away. Dung may be a renewable resource, but this cheap source of energy contributes tremendously to air pollution and respiratory health issues.

There are schools everywhere in India, imposing edifices protected by sturdy fences, signifying the value Indians give education. Many of the schools we saw appeared to be private, with a huge banner sweeping across the side of the building proclaiming the name and assuring potential patrons "English taught here." English is India's second official language, and widespread mastery of English has helped make Indians competitive in the international job market. Anyone who has spoken with someone in an Indian call center will recognize that Indian English is a dialect of its own.

In 2020, Prime Minister Narendra Modi announced the New Education Policy that included numerous reforms. For one, the plan purported to make public education more industry-oriented, focusing on "skilling" as well as conventional academics. The policy also put a greater emphasis on teaching primary school children in their mother tongue (mostly Hindi), rather than English. English would still be taught, but not used as the medium for instruction except in higher grades. As always with public education reforms, there was controversy.

About one-quarter of all Indian children attend private schools, which usually require uniforms. It was somewhat astonishing to see amidst the piles of rubble and the bullocks in the street and the vendors beside the road, a group of crisp and clean uniformed children walking to school. In fact, it was even more remarkable to see amidst the squalor men walking about in pressed white dishdashas. The women, too, *always* looked nice. They wore bright yellow or electric blue saris edged in beads or sequins, looking all dressed up even if they were doing manual labor or carrying cow dung on their heads.

How do they look so clean when sanitation and water are such big issues?

Bo and I discussed the cultural values that created various scenarios, for instance, the sight of a motor scooter weaving through traffic with an entire family aboard: Dad was driving, and he alone wore a helmet. Mom was sitting sidesaddle behind him with her hair covered by a scarf and her sari blowing in the wind. Two small children were squeezed between them. Perhaps we were reading too much into that vignette, but it seemed to represent a cross between the old cultural ways and the new economic energy of India.

The woman's genteel perch on the scooter reminded us of Ginger Rogers, Fred Astaire's dancing partner, who could dance every brilliant step he could…backwards and in high heels.

There is no concept of time among Indians. The thirty-minute drive to our stop for breakfast turned into almost two hours. Along the way, we stopped to pay a toll at the state line of Utter Pradesh. The cost to stay in Utter Pradesh for a full day was Rs. 260 ($5.20). How do they enforce that? we wondered. There was no exit toll.

As Arif got out to go inside the toll station, he warned us not to acknowledge the hawkers and vendors who would try very hard to sell us something.

"Monkeys on car. If you take picture, they are wanting money. Do not be opening the window or talking to them."

Sure enough. We sat in the locked car while a monkey climbed on the windshield and vendors banged on the window—*knock knock*. "Madam?"

We tried to watch what was going on without making eye contact. At last Bo laughed and said, "This is weird, sitting here trapped in monkey land."

It was awkward, to say the least. Yet we faced even more awkwardness at breakfast in Utter Pradesh.

We pulled into a roadside restaurant landscaped with many flowers and bushes in bloom amid the otherwise barren landscape. Inside we came face to face with a sort of shrine, a table with a large hand-cranked juicer and an immense pyramid of green-colored oranges. We were seated at a table with a commanding view of the shrine—an obvious point of pride for the owner. He waited on us himself, suggesting an American breakfast of omelet, toast with mixed jam, sweet coffee and—ta da—freshly squeezed orange juice.

In addition to admonitions not to drive in India, we had received firm warnings against drinking the water or eating anything that was not cooked. That included fresh fruit.

We cringed and tried to order canned juice but the owner was *so* proud of the squeezer, we felt guilty about declining and possibly hurting his feelings. So, being polite Southerners, we took the risk. In a sort of suicide pact, we agreed we both would do it. While breakfast was being prepared, we were treated to an elaborate orange-squeezing performance. The proprietor presented us full glasses with great flourish. We responded with many expressions of amazement and gratitude as we admired the glasses and sipped the contents through pursed lips. The juice was mild but tasty, and we assured the proprietor we had never tasted anything quite so delicious. Breakfast arrived and we turned our attention to food. Periodically, Bo would say in a sweet wheedling voice, "Finish all your juice."

When we emerged from the restaurant, wondering how long before we would pay the gastronomic price of drinking fresh fruit juice, we were met by a teenaged boy and a young girl in costume who wanted to entertain us. There was also a boy with a pair of monkeys on leashes doing tricks. We were told the boy had most likely simply captured young monkeys in the wild. We watched the song and dance routine and mused about living in a place where monkeys ran around like squirrels. After lavishing praise and applause on the youngsters, we consulted Arif about how much to tip them, then doubled it.

We may have been throwing the economy in disarray but no one was complaining. Americans are the biggest spenders we were told by several guides, but Americans quit coming to India after 9/11. Only now, ten years later, were they starting to return.

Arif, unsurprisingly, had a friend who was a guide at the Taj Mahal. We picked him up from a monument in the middle of a traffic circle in Agra. He was educated and quite knowledgeable and gave us a thorough tour.

At last we came to the Taj Mahal, that universal reference for huge palatial buildings, one of the seven manmade wonders of the world, the most famous thing about India, more famous even than *The Jungle Book* or Shiva or the slums of Mumbai, more famous than Gandhi or the Ganges or the call centers of Chennai. *The Taj.* After twenty-four hours of jet lag and culture shock, Bo and I recalled the purpose of our trip. As our guide led us into the compound, we grinned.

"Dad was here."

In June of 1944, Dad flew to Agra Air Base while on R&R following treatment in Ledo's 20th General Hospital for recurrent malaria and amoebic dysentery. Curious to see the world-famous landmark, he took a taxi to the Taj Mahal. He found the stunning building out in a field overlooking the muddy banks of the Yamuna River. No guide approached him. No ticket seller demanded payment. He wandered alone through the 17th century mausoleum and around the grounds, marveling that such a beautiful creation would be desecrated by trash and filth everywhere.

By the time Bo and I visited the Taj on our tour of Major Traywick's footsteps, the locals had recognized the financial value of tourism, and guides and photo ops and inlaid marble souvenirs were all available. Arif dropped us at the concession area where tourists can walk or catch a jitney to the actual compound. Next to the souvenir stands offering the usual fare were two elephants. *Have your picture taken on the pony.*

We were surprised to find, beyond the white building pictured in every travel brochure, the Taj is a complex that includes matching buildings on either side, a red sandstone gate almost as large as the Taj Mahal itself, as well as ancient quarters for the original construction artisans. Listening to our guide's earnest telling of much fascinating history, it dawned on us that he could not imagine anything comparable in the entire world. But many average Americans like us have seen, *par example,* Versailles, St. Paul's Cathedral, Machu Pichu, the Coliseum, and so we looked upon the Taj Mahal in that context. Nevertheless, we assured the guide, "I'm sure we'll talk about seeing the Taj Mahal the rest of our lives."

In keeping with the invisible network among Indians, Arif took every opportunity to encourage us to contribute to the Indian economy. His guide friend did, too. As we drove through the city following our tour of the Taj, one or the other would say, "The madam would be shopping now?"

I'd say no, we just like looking around.

"Jewels. The stones like the Taj Mahal. Silver. All finest jewelry. Cheap, very cheap."

Most people in India assumed Bo and I were married and it was convenient to let them think that. So I said, teasing, "No, he won't buy me any jewelry."

But they wouldn't give up.

"Agra is having the finest rugs. All handmade. Very cheap here."

I tried saying thank you but I couldn't carry a rug back. Wrong answer.

Arif and the guide perked up. *Oh is that all?* "Shipping rug, no problem. Very cheap."

And so it went.

Eventually, unbidden, they took us to a workshop where artisans inlaid semiprecious stones in marble, as we had seen at the Taj. A couple of old men crouched over makeshift tables under a tent roof in front of a building, cutting spaces into a piece of marble and fitting an intricate mosaic of semiprecious stones. We were made to understand that these skills are not being studied by the younger generation—a universal problem, Bo and I agreed.

We then toured the showroom and I wanted to buy an inlaid marble table because they were beautiful and, as Arif informed us, cheap. I couldn't make up my mind which one, but mostly I was worried about how to get it home. I had sense enough to realize I couldn't schlep a fifty-pound marble table top around India and Dubai for two weeks, and I had reservations about shipping it. Would it get there? In one piece? Shipping would probably cost more than the tabletop. Like a good sidekick, Sundance had my back: Bo did the rupee-dollar conversion and the tabletop I was planning to buy for $35 turned out to be $350. So I settled for a two-inch inlaid elephant, and we each bought something for Mom. I had a heck of a time explaining to the disappointed salesmen that I had misunderstood the price by a factor of ten. They were ready to haggle, but not down to $35.

Undeterred by our failure to buy a $350 marble tabletop, Arif stopped on the way back to Delhi at a restaurant with a large souvenir shop attached. Most notable about this stop was the sign by the door: "Do not visit the monkey or snake by the road. Not safe."

This was also the place where I went to the ladies' room and found a male attendant. The bathroom consisted of a large room with several stalls with doors, an extraordinary luxury in a country where most of the time I used a filthy cubicle with nothing but three walls around a hole in the ground. The attendant waited respectfully for me to emerge from a stall and wash my hands before approaching and offering me a paper towel. It was just one more cultural difference to be absorbed in our journey. It reminded me of one of Dad's first days at the military training camp at Ramgarh. The orderlies were Indian but they had been trained in British customs under the Raj. At the end of a hot day, Dad's orderly said, "Master, I have drawn your bath." Then he approached and began unbuttoning Dad's shirt, to which Dad reacted in shock. "What the hell are you doing?" he demanded.

The poor boy was confused. Dad was confused. Another cross-cultural misunderstanding.

The afternoon drive back to Delhi was just as hair-raising as the morning drive. Hurtling along at 90 km/hour (55 mph), we often felt Arif was playing chicken in the traffic with the oncoming vehicles. It was like watching a video game through the windshield with icons pelting the screen. No one gave any quarter, especially not our driver in an SUV. He honked at a small boy crossing the street with a large bundle and didn't slow down. Needless to say, there was no texting while driving. It was shocking enough that they could talk while driving.

We were speechless with fear all the way to Agra and most of the way back. At the hotel, babbling with relief to be alive, we showered Arif with rupees.

That night in the bar we threw caution to the wind and ordered ice for our drinks. At that point, we were long past worrying about the purity of the water in the ice cubes.

Chapter 6

In the Hill Country -- Darjeeling

March 17-18, 2011

The putative reason for this trip was to see where Dad went during the war so I could faithfully recreate the environment in my book about the family in World War II. But sometimes Bo and I got to having so much fun that we forgot about the mission. The hallowed Ledo Road was yet to come, and in the interim, the two days we spent in Darjeeling proved to be pure entertainment.

Darjeeling was on the itinerary because Dad often spoke of his training in Darjeeling at the British jungle warfare school. Darjeeling, as we learned when we got there, is a state as well as a city. It was one of those basic factoids that I might have known had I had the services of Dean King's research assistant. No wonder I had trouble finding the training camp. My own pre-trip research seemed to place the facility in the foothills east and south of the city, a location I could never pinpoint.

We did pass many remnants of military outposts on the flat land before climbing six thousand feet to the city and wondered if Dad had been there. Dad's training culminated in a three-day survival hike during which he ate wild bananas, slept near a herd of elephants and twice saw tigers cross his path—activities we did not experience on top of the mountain. Still, it was a valuable stop on the itinerary because Darjeeling is one of the old British hill stations. Dad had stayed at the hill station at Masoori. Staying at Darjeeling would give me a sense of what that was like.

Darjeeling is a city of more than 100,000 people hanging from the heights of the Himalayan foothills with no

connection to the rest of India except a narrow road with scores of switchbacks. The city did not start low and spread gradually up the mountainside. Darjeeling and other settlements along India's northern border—"hill stations"—were built from the top down as a refuge from the oppressive summer heat in the flatland. But there is no plateau or tableland for settlement. Up in the clouds at six or seven thousand feet, the buildings seem to cling to the steep hillsides by their fingernails. If you tripped and fell, there would be nothing but a few tea bushes and rhododendron to break your fall for six thousand feet.

Obviously the residents are acclimated to the terrain. We saw a soccer field cut into the side of the mountain. Remarkably, there was no fence or netting on the downhill side. There's a strong incentive for kids to learn ball control early.

According to Ashook, our driver, Darjeeling means "Queen of the Hills." But it is not a pretty city or, except in small spots, charming in its decline. It is dirty, like everything in India. The buildings are crowded together, clutching each other to keep from sliding down the slope, leaning this way and that. The ubiquitous billboards and signs advertising cell service add garish color, and over all, telephone and electric wires loop and hang like a widow's lacy shawl that has slipped off her shoulder and threatens to drag the ground.

"Twenty years ago Darjeeling was beautiful—rich and clean," Ashook told us. "Now too many buildings and pollution. Beautiful view now but everywhere you look there is a building. They are kicking their own stomach. If the tourist wasn't come in Darjeeling, we would die."

As we looked around, we couldn't help but agree, especially since the cloud cover ensured that we didn't even have the compensation of the (apparently) stunning view of the Himalayas.

As with Agra, getting there was half the thrill. The flight from Delhi to Siliguri was blessedly uneventful—probably the only time we could say that during the entire trip. Ashook met us at the airport for the three- or four-hour drive up the mountain. Despite being only 43 miles, the drive was so arduous that we paid him to stay on the mountain until our departure two days hence.

Fortunately, Arif had broken us in to the basics of Indian driving the day before. We had more of the same travel excitement, only this time we had the additional thrill of climbing six thousand feet on a rutted, 1 ½-lane packed gravel road with two-way traffic. And this route, we learned, was an improvement over taking the Cart Road.

The drive was slow but stimulating. There were scores of switchbacks requiring regular horn toots. Once again it was necessary to know the exact contours of one's car. We had the thrill of seeing, many times, the gap between a down-bound lorry and a pedestrian (often a small child in a uniform) narrow and close as we barreled toward them. Usually, the child casually stepped up onto the ten-inch wide concrete curb that separated the road from the abyss as the vehicles honked and zoomed past.

On one occasion we faced a head-on collision as two vehicles rolled down the mountain towards us side by side. By then we were veterans who could laugh in the face of such danger. I was high on three tabs of Bonine, in any case.

To my delight, our hotel turned out to be a charming, beautifully-maintained remnant of the British presence. The Mayfair mounts the hillside on multiple levels with porches overlooking the valley (we presumed, since the mountain was socked in for our entire visit). It is a cross between a Swiss chalet and an outpost of the colonial Empire, with red peaked roofs and not-quite-Victorian white gingerbread trim setting off the bright yellow exterior. Buddha, Persephone, Shiva, and the Virgin Mary are congregated in the ecumenical central garden, around which the hotel's private and public rooms swirl and rise or fall in steps. Five concrete rabbits, two squirrels and a flock of ducks decorate the grass, along with some incongruously kitsch animals: big round green pigs with bold red nostrils. When Katie Bo went to India in 2018 for a friend's wedding, I urged her to go to Darjeeling and stay at the Mayfair, which she agreed was one of the best parts of her trip. (That was saying a lot, since she had the luxury tour of Jaipur and Udaipur.)

The Mayfair provided a buffet for breakfast and supper, which relieved us of the challenge of figuring out where to eat. We were not recreating "Eat Pray Love," we just wanted to cover as much ground as possible with sustenance at appropriate intervals. Safely-cooked sustenance. We survived the freshly squeezed OJ episode unscathed, so in Darjeeling we decided to live dangerously—*more* dangerously—by brushing our teeth with tap water.

We walked uptown after we checked in and found a square with alpine village shops running off in a couple of directions. They were selling Indian brass hookahs and Hindu gods, not Ralph Lauren shirts and Fair Isle sweaters.

Bo was fascinated by all the Hindu, Buddhist and Eastern gods, and he perused the brass statuettes with a view to taking one (or more) home, if only he could make up his mind. To help with his decision, he bought "A Guide to Buddhist and Hindu Gods." He was leaning towards the Hindu god Ganesha, the god of happiness and prosperity. Apparently Hindus must pray to him first and then to whomever else they have a mind to worship. In the end, though, Bo bought a small figurine of Shiva, which today shares a place of honor on his mantle alongside Mary Magdalene, the Virgin Mary, Joseph and Little Baby Jesus.

He made his purchase in a tiny shop crowded with shelves of religious figurines in small, medium and large, as well as brass monkeys, tigers and elephants in dramatic poses, also available in small, medium and large. We chatted up the shopkeeper, whose grandfather had owned the place, which had been there more than a hundred years. Bo told him, "It might be that our father came into this shop."

Around the cobblestone square were mountain men with pathetic thin ponies available for photographs. I was comforted that they at least didn't have to go anywhere, just stand there with a child for photo. We spied low stone stables just off the square. No bedding of course, but a roof. One little chestnut was especially pathetic, pointing his right front in evident pain, resting the opposite hind foot. His hocks were touching, leaning together and forming a triangle that kept his hind end from falling down. He never moved the entire hour and a half we were in the area, and he limped off to his stable at dark.

Returning to the hotel, we saw two cats, the first of the trip. The dogs here show more genetic diversity than those in Delhi but the same apparent homelessness. Many black dogs, dogs with longer fur and floppy ears. I read some years back about an animal welfare outfit that had as its laudable goal neutering dogs in India. They have not made it to Delhi or Darjeeling yet.

Back in our room, which had a television, Bo surfed the non-English-speaking channels. We watched Hindustani commercials for awhile, trying to guess what the product was. After awhile Bo turned up the volume. "I wanted to hear what they were saying," he quipped.

Then he flipped through the channels and paused at a Japanese station presenting a news story—in Japanese, of course—about the Fukushima nuclear power plant. An earthquake caused a massive tsunami to strike Fukushima, Japan, just before we flew to India, but we did not know how devastating the event was. As we watched the stunning images, we longed to understand what the newscaster was saying.

Bo finally gave up on that and switched to what was apparently an Indian soap opera. Disappointed that the hero had more swash than buckle, he said, "You want to watch this?"

"No," I said, "I saw it last week: He gets the girl."

Eventually we found coverage of the cricket tournament, which, although it was in English, was equally unintelligible.

Day four was our first leisurely morning. We opted not to get up at four a.m. and go to the famed viewing spot at Tiger Hill to watch the sun rise over the Himalayas, partially because we didn't want to get up at four but mostly because the mountains were socked in. It was sort of a relief—although of course we were hoping it cleared before we left.

Around seven a.m., I was awakened by a series of crashes that I took to be the collapse of the entire wing next to us, but that turned out to be a herd of monkeys playing on the corrugated metal roof. Think twenty-pound squirrels.

They ran along the railings of the multi-level chalet-style hotel and leaped from gutter to roof, racing back and forth and playing, occasionally squealing like fighting cats. I took a picture of one just outside the window.

Down in the courtyard half a dozen Japanese staff members came out to investigate. The monkeys, unintimidated by people, rushed to the pergola where the men stood and the men quickly retreated. No one wants to get bitten by a monkey. They carry rabies and other diseases.

In a moment the men returned armed with umbrellas, and two courageous souls leaped up at the roof and attempted to drive the monkeys away with flailing umbrellas. Quite a sight.

I got up and sat before the picture window in our cozy garret room, looking out at the range of mountains over which a curtain of mist had been drawn. Bo was in the lobby or somewhere, and I was in my pjs drinking tea and eating biscuits, wonderful crackers with chives. From somewhere outside came the odd mixturc of car horns and roosters crowing.

Beyond the hotel I could see several spines of the mountain successively fading into the mist. At night they were thickly dotted with lights, like sequins sprinkled on the mountaintop instead of snow. Even with the memory of the number of lights on the mountainside, I was surprised in the morning to see how thickly settled the nearby slopes were. Our driver told us there were ten "lakhs" living on top of the "hill," a lakh being a number he couldn't translate but that we initially worked out to be 10,000. Actually, it is 100,000, making for a population of one million people spread across the mountaintop, a number that still seems astonishing.

Just to the left was an old stone half-timbered house that must have once been quite beautiful. On most of the rooftops sat big casks of water, each about the size of four 55-gallon drums but taller. A cask holds five hundred liters and, according to Ashook, lasts his household of eight people three days. Laundry was hanging everywhere, like the ubiquitous Buddhist prayer flags strung across gorges or mounted on poles. A Buddhist is supposed to put up a display of prayer flags behind his house, and this is Buddhist territory.

All down the hillside and between houses were enormous brilliant red rhododendron in bloom, many broad-leafed evergreens, and pines with long, textured needles. There was the occasional clump of banana plants. With ragged and winter-burned leaves, they looked like nature's reflection of the Buddhist prayer flags. Surprisingly at this elevation, the temperature rarely falls below freezing, although it does snow occasionally.

We spent the morning poking around a monastery in Ghoom, not THE Ghoom Monastery that is officially open for tours, just some smaller cousin that we more or less barged into by mistake.

First we went to the railroad station to buy tickets on the "toy train" as far as Ghoom. This little train looks like something children would ride around a very small amusement park. It runs right along the street all the way up to Darjeeling from the flats, but it takes ten hours, which is why we had hired a car. Still, we thought it would be fun to ride four or five miles to Ghoom.

At the station, we randomly got in a line and waited awhile, even though the lines were not moving. We could see two men inside the ticket windows doing paperwork and making no effort to speak to the waiting customers. This led us to believe, naively, that the customers ahead of us had already been told what was happening, whatever that was. Eventually Bo went in search of help. He returned with the news that (1) they couldn't sell tickets because the internet was down and (2) all the trains were full anyway. So we got a taxi from the line nearby.

The driver dropped us at the top of a ramp that led down into the courtyard of a monastery and that was lined with a gauntlet of women selling pashmina wool shawls. We were beset by the saleswomen and politely studied all their wares. Some had better quality goods than others. As we looked at one's pile, another would approach and try to entice us to look at her pile. Finally, we gave them to understand that we would shop when we came out of the monastery.

Then we wandered around what appeared to be an abandoned place consisting of a temple in the middle of the courtyard and a semi-circular building jutting out over the edge of the cliff. The monastery is a three- or four-story building built in a curve around the shoulder of the mountain. It appears to be mostly one room deep, so that the rooms have a door on the inner courtyard and windows out over the mountainside. There is no glass in the windows. While it rarely snows here, it does get down in the thirties, so life is rather Spartan.

As we walked around the temple, we saw a small dog asleep in some brush and a line of water faucets in the open that made me shudder on this cool morning. We even went down some open stairs in the monastery and out through an archway to the back, overlooking the steep mountainside covered with rhododendron, brush, trash and tea plants. When we went back to the courtyard, a monk showed up and talked to us.

He invited us into the temple, which was dominated by an enormous Buddha, maybe ten feet tall, gilded and painted in bright reds and blues, surrounded by elaborate shrines, paintings and icons, each with complex religious significance. In front of the Buddha stood a wide altar piled with braids and sticks of bread, flanked by a small stack of literature, boxes of incense and an alms box.

The monk wrote his name in my notebook – Ngawang Chodar. When he learned we were American he said he had been to America. “Berman.”

Berman. We looked at each other and struggled to understand because he was so proud and it was obviously important for us to know where he had been. He finally said he had been to the Catskills, where the monastery has a branch. Then we realized he was referring to Vermont!

Having never met a Buddhist, we were interested to learn about his life and the life of the monastery. The main temple is in Tibet. This branch in Darjeeling, built in 1952, is one of four branches in India. The date is significant because China annexed the independent nation of Tibet in 1951, wresting control from the Dalai Lama, renaming it the Tibet Autonomous Region and sending in ethnic Han Chinese to snuff out Tibetan culture. It seems likely Tibetan families have been supporting the Indian branches as a way to maintain Tibetan culture in exile.

Fifty-two people live at the monastery, of which thirty-seven are students, young boys from India and the surrounding area, which includes Bhutan and Tibet. It is a two-year program

PLEASE REMOVE SHOES
SMOKING IS STRICKLY PROHIBITED

of traditional and religious education. After two years, each boy decides whether to stay or leave. I tried to imagine the parents in Bhutan who would send their son to boarding school here. Virginia Episcopal School this is not. Are the families prosperous or poor? Is this choice similar to European life in the days of primogeniture when the second son often went into the priesthood? Or, given the appropriation of Tibet by China, I wonder if Tibetan families send their sons to Darjeeling to escape Chinese assimilation.

The monastery makes money with a café and by selling incense. They make their own incense from a recipe in the prayer book, using sandal root, saffron, sweet shrub, cardamom, cloves, and twigs from a small kind of rhododendron. They use a press to make the incense, but it must be done in hot weather, presumably when the flora are fresh and full of juice.

They also have cows at some location outside town—we tried to imagine a herd on this steep hillside. They produce seventy kilograms of milk daily, which the monks use to make various dairy products.

Eventually the monk—actually, the abbot—invited us into the café, ordered tea and gave us some of the ceremonial bread. The bread is made on some holiday and then laid before the altar for a month before it is eaten. It *was* pretty crispy but did not taste like month-old bread.

The visit was fascinating from a cultural standpoint, but I realized later that we had learned nothing about Buddhist theology. I had to go home and read later about the practice of self-denial and meditation leading to nirvana. There are branches of Buddhism, the most famous one being the branch from Tibet known as Lamaism, led by the Dalai Lama. The current Dalai Lama has lived in exile in India since 1959. And then there is the Burmese branch. As I write this in 2023, I have been mystified and horrified by the brutality of the Buddhist monks in Burma who have engaged in ethnic cleansing against the Rohingya Muslims in northwest Burma, killing thousands and driving hundreds of thousands into Bangladesh and Malaysia.

As Bo and I bid the abbot goodbye, we left a relatively generous gift, mainly because we had no small bills. A hundred rupees—about two dollars—would have been sufficient, but we had nothing smaller than a five hundred-rupee note. As in many other cultural situations, Bo and I felt we had received more reward than any tip or gift we presented. Suitably educated in monastery life and properly blessed, we ventured forth on our next adventure.

The mountains were still shrouded in clouds, so we assuaged our disappointment by shopping for pashminas. The ladies on the ramp outside the monastery were undoubtedly pleased. We haggled a bit for show, but quickly settled for prices ranging from four to eight dollars apiece. We bought eight, careful to buy at least one from each table. Several were allegedly gifts for Mom and my friends, and ultimately, I did manage to part with a few of them, but the brilliant colors and detailed workmanship made it hard for me to give them up.

There was no taxi line outside the monastery so we walked several miles. After we finally broke a five hundred-rupee note at a gas station, some man offered to drive us to the hotel for one hundred rupees and we accepted.

We walked many kilometers up and down the narrow, steep streets of Darjeeling. The altitude is about 6,700 feet, but we handled it okay. More difficult was trying to follow a two-dimensional map in such a three-dimensional town. As we wandered around, we looked for an ATM. Very challenging. Half the time my card didn't work and we had to drain Bo's account. One time I got enough change to spend fifteen minutes at an internet café.

Bo and I had decided against buying or renting an international cell phone, an expensive option at that time. We would be together the entire trip, for one thing. For another, we figured we could find an occasional business office and send a reassuring email back home. That was an optimistic assumption, as it turned out. For the eight days between Delhi and Calcutta, we were largely out of touch with the outside world, so my husband Cricket unfortunately remained in the dark and anxious about our safety and whereabouts most of the time. We weren't anxious, because *we* knew we were okay, but it was often a challenge to get that message out in a land where continuous power is an oxymoron, wires hang like spaghetti and 3G stands for Gandhi, Ganges and Ganesha.

After returning from the monastery excursion, Bo and I walked downhill to the zoo and had a long climb back to the hotel, but like everything else, it was worth it.

In 2022, India's Central Zoo Authority rated the Padmaja Naidu Himalayan Zoological Park in Darjeeling the best zoo in India, among 150 zoos. Founded in 1958 as a place to study and preserve Himalayan fauna, the zoo has a well-regarded breeding program for certain endangered species. The zoo has a wide collection of Himalayan animals and keeps on display such endangered species as snow leopards, red pandas, Tibetan wolves, goral mountain goats and several species of birds—all in natural habitats.

We saw a snow leopard run and leap around the rocks in his cage. What a beautiful animal. His agility was astonishing. He would be in one spot and then he'd appear on top of the rocks so fast you couldn't see him move. His tail was quite long and seemed to have a thicker hunk at the end—he used it as a tightrope walker uses a balance bar. I feel blessed to have seen such an animal but I did feel sorry for him in captivity. Knowing the zoo is breeding snow leopards and others was an encouraging thought.

The park has a big aviary that holds many exotic birds with brilliant-colored plumage. To think such gorgeous creatures inhabit the earth! I love our little brown wrens, but their contribution to the beauty of the world isn't their appearance, it's the arresting tremolo of their song.

We had a good time watching the red pandas. They are too cute for words, sort of a cross between a raccoon and a bear. Native

to the eastern Himalayans, they are endangered, with fewer than 10,000 animals remaining.

The zoo had a cage with Tibetan wolves, a must in the land of Mowgli. The park at one time had two Siberian tigers, a 1960 gift of Soviet Premier Nikita Khrushchev. We did not see a tiger on our visit to the park in 2011, but apparently they have tigers now.

Tigers are my favorite animal in the world and they are severely endangered, with only about four thousand left in the wild—half of them in India. There are actually more tigers in captivity than in the wild. I was appalled to learn in the course of reading Dane Huckelbridge's "No Beast So Fierce" how the British colonials thoroughly disrupted the tigers' environment in India and then proceeded to hunt the big cats nearly to extinction. Of course, at about the same time, Americans were hunting bison and wolves into the ground. Even though humans have learned from those mistakes, there are still parts of the world where large animals are threatened by humans: giraffes, elephants and big cats are all struggling to maintain their populations in parts of Africa. So it is encouraging to know how much India supports and promotes the tiger populations scattered around the country. India does more to maintain tigers in the wild than any other country, and significantly, the tiger population has been growing at about five percent a year since 2006.

I was at that moment hoping to see a tiger in the wild at Kaziranga National Park, our next stop, so not seeing one at the zoo was okay.

Darjeeling is home to the Bengal Natural History Museum. We sought out the museum, drawn by the chief advertised feature: a giant leech. Dad talked a lot about leeches in India and Burma, so this was a must-see attraction. The giant leech did not disappoint. It was indeed an enormous bloated thing in a jar of formaldehyde. We oohed and ahhed over it appreciatively. Then we examined the other dead things, spiders, insects, butterflies and a few moth-eaten mammals. The museum is a relic of the Raj, an artifact in and of itself. It is a small dusty building with low ceilings and items presented in old-fashioned glass cases. The typed cards of identification and the displays themselves appear untouched for what? Fifty? Sixty? Seventy years?

I sent Katie Bo in search of the giant leech when she went to Darjeeling, but she found only a modern museum with no such exhibit. I suspect the old museum is still tucked away at the end of a street, because what else would they do with a giant leech?

As we wandered through the streets looking for the Natural History Museum, we came upon some children playing cricket. The ball came rolling to us and Bo picked it up. Then he approached the batter and bowled the ball. The batter hit it and Bo caught it, leading to cheers and shouts from the children. But the second time he bowled, we missed catching the hit, while the batter ran and the other children shrieked in delight.

Bo and I watched the world championship tournament whenever we found a TV and continued trying to figure out the rules. India was playing New Zealand in the final round(s), so the

tournament was the talk of the nation. We often drove past children out in barren fields playing cricket with make-shift bats and balls. At night, we sat for hours in bars all over the country, drinking and watching incomprehensible activity on the TV, all the while making hilariously ill-informed commentary. I hope we didn't offend anyone around us.

That day, the BBC reported that the clouds were moving East, giving us the hope we could at last see the mountains before we descended in the morning. When the skies are clear, Mount Kangchenjunga supposedly stands as a snow-covered beacon high above the rest of its neighbors. It is the third highest peak in the Himalayan range, after Everest and K-2.

Despite the allure of seeing the Himalayas on a clear day, the twin goals of the trip were still to come, the Ledo Road and the jungle. To reach those goals, we had first to take a long trip that would test our endurance: three hours hurtling down the mountain from Darjeeling to Bagdogra, a two-hour flight to Guwahati, and five more gut-wrenching hours on the road to Kaziranga National Park.

I was trying to follow Dean King's advice to *go there*, to see what the jungle looks and smells like. The national park was the best substitute for seeing the Burmese jungle that I could come up with beyond reading Tarzan books.

I was planning to see the jungle, even if the trip on Indian roads killed me.

But I was really hoping to see a tiger.

CHAPTER 7

LOOOOONG TRAVEL DAY

March 19, 2011

We had several of those but this was one of the longest, exacerbated, of course, by the stress of riding in a car lurching through traffic: Two hours down off the mountain plus an hour more to the airport, the flight from Bagdogra to Guwahati, the five-hour drive to Kaziranga.

A long day of nothing but travel should make for a short chapter, but in fact driving through India, looking at the countryside, talking to our drivers and guides proved to be instructive and interesting as always. However, it left very little time to do anything else. Except for watching cricket on TV in the bar late at night.

It was in Darjeeling that we first heard about the upcoming elections. These regional contests are held at five-year intervals, so there was a great deal of enthusiasm and debate and, in some areas, agitation. The day we left Darjeeling, the state governor was coming to visit, so, like the three wise men, we departed by a different way. Ashook drove us down the mountain on a more scenic but narrower (if possible) track.

Amazingly, he managed to entertain and educate us despite the challenges of negotiating traffic on the steep twisting road, a two-hour trip that made "The Man from Snowy River" look like a trot through Central Park.

Along the way, we passed endless kilometers of sloping tea fields. In fact, tea bushes were growing all over the steepest hillsides from Darjeeling to the flat land. I don't see how they pick the leaves without falling down the mountain. Ashook told us they picked all the leaves but that the small ones on top were the best. "They use everything."

Whipping around hairpin turns and dodging Tata Sumas with sixteen passengers, Ashook said, "My father doesn't want me to learn to drive but I [was determined]. Now when I take my parents to Siliguri, they are happy." Apparently his parents enjoy riding around in his air-conditioned car in the summer.

He said he had only one month in which to learn to drive, which may explain a lot about the driving in India. Although I feel certain something has been lost in the translation here, Ashook told us the instructor incentivized him to learn quickly by hitting him with a jack handle when he made a mistake.

Tata is an Indian auto maker. They make trucks as well as a Tata Nano—a small car "like a golf cart" Ashook said. The smallest car costs 100,000 Rs., about $2,000. On the high end, Ashook told us, "Toyota Camry is what rich peoples buy."

Ashook was very forthcoming about the national culture of graft. As we passed people fixing the road, he said, "After the rainy season, they are having to fix it all again. The government pays the contractor ten lakhs, the contractor invests three lakhs to fix the road and keeps seven lakhs."

And later: "In India, if you are getting a job, you have to pay a lot of money to the official getting you the job."

Just three years after our visit, Narendra Modi was elected prime minister on a pledge to fight corruption. His efforts have yielded some observable progress, but rooting out a culture of graft takes a long time. Since Bo and I were there, India has slowly moved up Transparency International's corruption index to a middle rank of 80, but the country's overall score has been stagnant. I interpret that to mean that India's corruption level is still the same, but other countries have gotten worse.

Once down on flat land, Bo and I saw workshops and vendors in clumps along the road, sort of like a strip mall. One open shed seemed to be the factory for hand-made teakwood bedsteads, furniture that looked solid and attractive. Do the pieces get shipped to American stores? At another shed nearby, we saw a cow waiting in line at a shop for lunch.

Sign on a ramshackle building: Computerized auto pollution testing facility. (Do they test to make sure the cars *are* polluting?)

Sign by the road: Don't fly but ply. (Go ahead but don't speed.)

At the Bagdogra Airport, there seemed to be a lot more security than we had seen previously: Men in uniforms walking around carrying rifles in their hands, at the ready, not slung over their shoulders. We were in the northeast and going deeper into India's outback, where political agitators were stirring up trouble in advance of the elections.

Also, the security routine was different. First we sent our bags through a check point. They were carry-on bags, but we weren't allowed to retrieve them. Then we sat in a waiting area. We were not sure what would happen next so we got distracted and talked and read. Suddenly we heard through the airport hub-bub the loudspeaker calling our names! We hadn't heard the original boarding call for our flight and they don't wait around there. We ran to a gate and men with guns directed us through to security. We were sent into separate curtained cubicles for a pat down, mine by a woman in full burqa. Somewhere we got our bags and walked out onto the tarmac to get on the plane.

We sat for awhile on the tarmac, then they unloaded the plane. They told us we could leave our luggage on board, but we chose to take ours with us. Who knew what would happen next and we did not want to be separated. They led us back inside the terminal. Eventually they loaded us on the plane again—without repeating the security routine. Oh well. They had guns. I'm sure we were safe.

As we ascended through the clouds and saw, for the first time in days, blue sky, we also saw Kangchenjunga, the 28,000-foot peak allegedly visible from Darjeeling. Flying above the clouds, we could see the Himalayas stretching out to the west, sharp and capped with snow dripping down like icing, not a solid line of peaks, just clumps of peaks sticking up through the clouds here and there, with the big boy dominating, of course.

A man in his thirties sat next to us and told us about his life. He had a good job, he was attractive and he was single but thought his prospects of marriage were slim because he had no family to arrange a match. He was clearly locked in a cultural conundrum. It was sad.

Even with our tardiness in Bagdogra, the plane arrived early at Guwahati and our tour guide and driver weren't around yet. I had found this car and driver online, and we experienced a few moments of wonder about whether we would be stranded in Guwahati.

However, they soon showed up—Budyudd, a young earnest educated tour guide, and Chandrum, the well-dressed, non-English-speaking driver.

Bud, as he asked to be called, and I had a lengthy discussion of the finances, which had never been settled because before we left, I switched the nature park booking from Manas to Kaziranga, which affected the lodging rate as well as the transportation rate. Then there was the issue of the exchange rate. I had my paperwork and he had his. It was all very civil and with help from Sundance, we sorted out the discrepancies—all in their favor, of course. We owed them 5541 Rs – about $120.

Planning an a la carte trip like this one made me appreciate the value of a professional travel agency. The biggest challenge was figuring out how long it would take to get from one place to another. For some of the longer legs, we flew. I wanted to take the train somewhere, just for the experience, but too many people wrote or spoke of the unreliability of train schedules in India. Sometimes a train is five hours late, sometimes two days. We couldn't afford such uncertainty in our itinerary. Additionally, the trains to the far northeast of West Bengal and into Assam had been attacked by bandits during recent periods of unrest. We had no way to judge the level of risk, so we stuck to private cars and airplanes.

My main source of information about conditions on the ground and local travel advice was IndiaMike.com, a message board for travelers in India, mostly written by and geared towards Indian natives—still a useful site when I checked recently. I read many threads about Assam and its sister states, mainly Arunachal Pradesh, and corresponded with several posters about their travels. Many of the latter had backpacked around on public transit and stayed in the Indian equivalent of youth hostels. Bo and I were going economy, but we didn't want to get bogged down trying to figure out bus schedules nor did we want to camp out. Still, the postings gave me an idea of what to expect. Through IndiaMike, I found helptourism.com, an eco-tourism outfit promoting travel in that area and through which I booked cars, drivers and accommodations for the four most important days of the trip: Kaziranga Park to Ledo to…the border of Burma? (The helptourism.com site is still accessible and has working links to other sites, but the site itself appears to be stale.)

Interestingly, all these travel arrangements were made and carried out without credit cards, either in advance or on site. Other than wiring money for the reservation at Diphlu River Lodge outside Kaziranga Park, we settled up in cash in person. And it all worked.

Chandrum had a nice car, which was good because we spent a lot of time in it, mostly terrified. I would surely have been carsick a hundred times a day had I not been fortified with double doses of Bonine, which I was taking twice a day by then. It's not curvy roads but braking that causes me to be nauseated, and normal driving in India consists of flooring the gas pedal to dart into a hole followed by mashing on the brake when the hole fills up with a Tata truck.

By the time we got to Guwahati, we were prepared for the fact that it would take five hours to get to Kaziranga, even though it is only about 140 miles *and* they have a partially-completed dual-lane highway. Emphasis on "partially". The problem with the highway is that it has been built in dozens of short sections of two or three miles with sometimes-lengthy gravel sections in between. The paved sections end abruptly, with no gravel or dirt slope to ease the transition. So, the car rolls carefully up the four-inch vertical face to get on the concrete road, the driver mashes the gas and hurtles along at 60 mph for three minutes then jams on the brake, coming to a standstill before easing off the four-inch drop to the gravel. Then the car grinds along in the gravel and dust and occasional pothole sometimes for fifty yards, sometimes long enough to reach a speed of 20 or 30 mph, before reaching another section of paved road. The paved section may be the left side or the right side, but vehicles use them indiscriminately. Eventually we got to some places where the pavement was good for as much as five miles. But still this was only one side, so we were dodging rickshaws and trying to pass 1950s lorries without hitting the oncoming bus or truck.

They told us the road was due to be finished in 2008. It was now 2011. In 2013, the Indian government announced a massive infusion of funds into highway construction for the area. And in 2023…

Bo and I dealt with the constant fear of death by cracking wise. The truth was, beyond the black humor, we had a grand rollicking fun time together exploring an exotic country and being gob-smacked by cultural differences every hour of every day. It was always interesting when we persuaded our guides to talk to us about life in India.

We asked Bud and Chandrum what would happen if you hit a cow. Bud said, "Oh that would be terrible! The owner comes and you can't leave until you pay. If a female cow, the owner will say pregnant and you have killed that one too. So it is 20,000 Rs. If a bullock, that is worse because more valuable. They are using them in the fields [to plow]. 40,000 Rs." (About $250 at that time.)

Our previous driver, Ashook, had told us if you hit a cow, you have to pay the owner 7,000-8,000 Rs. I guess the market is different in Darjeeling. If you hit something at night, Ashook said you don't stop. One time he hit a hen as he was taking two tourists to the airport. They didn't have time to stop. "The owner catch me on the way back. I pay 500 rupees ($3) for the hen. I want to take the hen home but she says she fixed it and have it."

Bud and Chandrum tried to give us a better than average level of service, stopping at attractive (in relative terms) restaurants and gas station/pit stops. That day we had lunch at the Tandoor Bar and Restaurant, which boasted a finished floor and finished walls, as well as a dining room with windows with glass instead of shutters. I don't know how we knew what we were ordering, but I had pigeon, according to my notes, and Bo had fish—"budhi"—wonderful tiny sardine-type fish fried all crispy. We had them several times and they were delicious.

Then I negotiated the toilet facilities, always a logistical challenge.

We had been advised that when traveling in India, one should carry toilet paper, but in fact moist wipes are better and easier to carry. I finally developed a working system by hanging my day pack around my neck—you don't want to set your bag down anywhere and needless to say, there's no convenient hook. Sometimes when you close the door, it's dark, adding to the problem of squatting while holding moist wipes, balancing the swinging day pack and trying to keep the hems of your pants from touching the floor. I always felt like I needed a handicapped rail and Shiva's two extra arms.

At first, I was mystified by the western toilets whose seat was fixed and consisted of porcelain treads. Then when I saw a few ladies' rooms with nothing but a hole in the floor flanked by treads in the shape of footprints, I remembered in this part of the world women squat and if confronted with a western toilet, they are even more challenged than I.

We arrived at Diphlu River Lodge at 7:30 p.m. after a bone-jarring vomit-inspiring five-hour drive from Guwahati airport. They were glad to see us but not half as glad as we were to be there. It was dark and a nice young lady served us guava juice on the porch of the gatehouse while Bud got us checked in. After being shown to our *basha*, we went next door to the *manchu*—the dining hall and public rooms—where we had a drink and delightful conversation with Bijoy Baruah, the manager. Bijoy treated us with fabulous hospitality throughout our stay.

He laid out a busy but exciting day for us at Kaziranga National Park—Up at four a.m. to take an elephant safari, then breakfast at the park followed by a jeep safari and home at noon. After lunch, another jeep safari to another section of the park. At last, I would be seeing "the jungle," with all the towering trees and vines, the elephant grass in the marshes, the exotic birds, monkeys and roaming herds of wild buffalo, deer and elephants. And maybe, if we were very lucky, a tiger.

We signed on for the full deal. *Dean, we are going there.*

After drinks, we were ready for bed, as it was 8:30 and we'd been traveling all day, but they had prepared dinner for us and were clearly eager to show us every accommodation, so we dined.

On our 2010 trip to Australia, Cricket and I frequently ate dinner late and then went straight to bed, where I had difficulty sleeping because dinner sat like a rock in my gut. In India the food was mostly vegetarian and certainly not rich, so that was not a problem.

Dinner involved rice with many different dishes to spread on top. The young man who took care of us was very eager to serve. They had a banquet table with six or eight covered steamer trays, all just for us because the other guests had eaten earlier. We filled our plates and enjoyed a delicious meal while they fussed over us just enough to make us feel we had gone back in time to the British Raj. We decided Dad would approve.

We also decided we could get used to this. Sundance, who is something of an ascetic, was being corrupted to a life of luxury. When I asked him about that, he said he was *way* beyond corrupted!

After praising the chef, the maître d' and the servers profusely, we took the occasion to hand over a couple of bags of laundry, so we would be fixed for the rest of the trip. We left home one week ago and return home one week from today.

A boy with a torch waited at the ready to light our way back to our *basha*. Our lodge was as advertised, a bamboo and thatch-looking westernized free-standing cabin on stilts overlooking the Diphlu River, a tributary of the mighty Brahmaputra River. The interior was luxurious by local standards, a large room with tasteful scatter rugs and coordinated bedspreads and window dressing. The shower had glass on two opposing sides, the far side of which was open to the outdoors with bushes like oleander providing some cover. A woven bamboo screen stood beyond the bushes. I gushed over the design, saying, "It's giving you the illusion you are showering outside."

Bo the wit replied, "It's giving the illusion you are showering in private."

Whatever. The water felt mighty good after a long day.

CHAPTER 8

INTO THE JUNGLE -- KAZIRANGA AND DIPHLU LODGE

March 20, 2011

Dad's introduction to the jungle came through a two-week training program at the British jungle warfare school somewhere in the state of Darjeeling. The course culminated in a three-day survival hike through terrain similar to Kaziranga Park, during which he ate wild bananas ("mostly seeds"), strained mosquito larvae out of standing water to make tea, crossed paths with tigers, and slept by a stream where wild elephants were watering.

Sadly, our guide could not recreate that entire experience for us, but he did his best.

As befits a large nature preserve, Kaziranga Park is in a rural state—Assam—and covers thousands of acres along the southern bank of the great Brahmaputra River. Visiting the park, which is only a few hundred miles from North Burma as the crow flies, was a perfectly good substitute for tracing Dad's exact footprints. In some ways, portions of our trip became as much an homage to Dad as a research mission. The sojourn at Diphlu River Lodge was one of those times.

When our wakeup call came—a knock on the door at four a.m.—we were already up and dressed. Again a boy lit our way and we walked across the bamboo bridge to the reception center, where our naturalist and guide, Pobitro—"Pobby"—and our driver picked us up. We drove fifteen minutes in the dark down Rt. 37 to the park entrance.

There we parked and walked a short way to "Boarding Station 1" for our safari ride on an elephant. Like much of the trip, we got to have fun doing the research on Dad's life in war. I think that in itself was revelatory of Dad's experience, because he clearly had an exciting time himself when he wasn't getting shot at.

Dad was curious about everything, and when his unit captured some logging elephants at Shwegu on the Irrawaddy River, he took an interest in the animals. He had been issued a chunk of opium to use for barter with the natives, and he cut a corner off and traded it for an elephant ride. An experienced horseman, he told us elephants had "a seasick walk." Maybe we had better seats, but it didn't seem so bad to me. Dad's ride included mounting a kneeling elephant and nearly being tossed when the elephant lurched to his feet, an experience we missed.

The captured elephants and their reputed intelligence intrigued him. He had occasion to see an elephant at work moving

teak logs. "That elephant slid his tusks under the log, then he gave it a little heft to see if it was balanced. If it wasn't, he put it down and moved over and tried again until he had it right." Dad was impressed by that. He would have loved reading Vicki Croke's "Elephant Company" about the working animals caught between the Allies and the Japanese in Burma in World War II.

Dad's elephants ended up in Taiwan when the Nationalist Chinese withdrew to the island, and years later he ran across a newspaper photograph of two of them, then in the Taipei Zoo and posing with wedding couples in a group ceremony,

So Bo and I were eager to have an elephant ride through the jungle. We were the first to arrive at the station, and we enjoyed watching the mahouts tacking up the elephants. It was just like tacking up a horse, except I don't make Bucky kneel down while I'm doing it.

They throw a saddle pad on his back, then add the saddle, which looks like the back seat of a station wagon with plaid flannel upholstery. Then ropes for a girth. Two men pull tight, one on top and one on the ground. Then a crupper, then a breastplate.

The mounting block is a large circular platform about eight feet off the ground. The elephant comes alongside and you get on. In lieu of stirrups, there's a running board—literally a board hanging by rope. The mahout perches in front of the saddle and uses voice commands as well as a stick or kicks the elephant's ears to guide him.

Once they were tacked up, the elephants were taken for water at a stream nearby. Two elephants had small babies that we were surprised to learn were four years old. One came to investigate the tourists. "Babu." Then a Jack Russell puppy approached the baby elephant and barked and the elephant retreated, to the amusement of the tourists. The puppy advanced until a man called him off.

By then it was just getting light and a dozen other tourists arrived.

We had the ride on Britanny, who has big tusks. Rumtunny was our mahout and he was very good—always had me in good position for photographs. I think the other tourists took pix of the back of my head.

Half a dozen elephants bearing eager tourists strode across a burnt-over field of elephant grass. The grass is the main forage for many of the park animals, and burning stimulates new growth.

We saw two samdar deer with fawns and some hog deer, their tawny coats well-camouflaged in the morning twilight. When we got into the tall elephant grass, great grey lumps moved about in the cover—rhinos! The one-horned rhinoceros is quite rare and most of the ones left in the world live at Kaziranga. They are pretty damn big and imposing, so we were glad to be on something bigger.

We saw one with a baby and I can attest that baby rhinos are cute. A big male posed for us, calmly sizing up the elephants. He was not as cute as the baby.

It started to rain, but Pobby had fitted us with umbrellas and we wore rain tarps of our own. Bo sat behind me and held the umbrella so I could shoot pix (in the dusk of pre-dawn). All around us people with umbrellas sat on elephants, a silly scene that somehow brought to mind Little Black Sambo with his parasol and shoes that the tigers stole. Would we be blessed with a tiger view?

After about an hour, our elephants unloaded us at "Station 2," where other tourists awaited our mounts. It was still only 6:30 a.m., and Pobby took us to a picnic breakfast at the interpretation station—tea, cheese sandwiches on excellent homemade white bread, hardboiled egg, and the ubiquitous bottled water.

The facilities at the station resembled a western commode, so I foolishly expected not to have any problems. I didn't have my usual supplies, but fortunately I had some tissues, since there was no paper. They don't use paper. They use a cup of water, which was also unavailable. Then I poked around looking for how to flush, to no avail, but I touched things, which made me uneasy. We did not then or ever get Delhi-belly so maybe we were lucky. Or maybe having grown up in the rural South where you "eat a peck of dirt before you die," we were sufficiently resistant to germs.

It rained some more, and we laughed at the people on the elephants coming in from the second shift in the pouring rain. When it let up, we went out on jeep safari for almost five hours. It rained off and on for the first half, and the boys put the top down and up. Then it rained so hard it was coming in the sides and we had to zip down the sides. We found ourselves riding along in the jeep, enclosed by curtains with no windows. We could see the puddles in front of the jeep through the windshield and that was it for about twenty minutes.

To quote Dad on the monsoon: "It would rain like hell for about twenty minutes, then it would stop. You'd be soaking wet, but then the heat would dry you off."

Finally, I unzipped the cover on my side and looked out, just to see the countryside. Eventually it stopped and we threw the side curtains up on the roof. By the end of the morning, we had the top down again and the sun was drying us off. We had some good laughs with Pobby, as we made jokes and he made jokes and we mostly understood each other.

Weather aside, the safari was a fabulous blur of animals, both individuals and herds. At one point we passed quite close to a herd of water buffalo who, like us, were waiting out the showers. All about in the trees and standing in the marshes and flying overhead we saw fabulous gold and green and blue and red colored birds—all the gorgeous birds of the Darjeeling zoo's aviary and more.

Driving through a broad open area towards a watchtower, the jeep suddenly stopped. Pobby had spied there beside the road a rock python, as big around as my thigh. He was slithering out of a hole and disappearing in the brush. We were in Kipling country and I thought of my favorite tale from "The Just So Stories," in which "the bi-coloured-python-rock-snake uncoiled himself very quickly from the rock and spanked the Elephant's Child with his scalesome, flailsome tail." Alas, we glimpsed only about six feet of the slick mottled serpent as he disappeared, not his scalesome, flailsome tail.

The sun was blazing when we climbed the watchtower and joined other tourists looking out over a huge savannah full of game. Elephants watered at the Diphlu River. Water buffalo loafed on the muddy bank or rooted around. Deer and warthogs grazed the broad expanse of grass. It was awesome and humbling to have this glimpse of herds of animals living peaceably, at the moment, in the wild. As we marveled at the scene, a herd of deer on the far side of the river suddenly bolted. Pobby and the other guides grabbed their binoculars. Was it a tiger frightening the game?

Inspired by the distraction, I guess, several women in saris took the opportunity to relieve themselves at the bottom of the watchtower.

Pobby didn't see a tiger, alas. Returning to the jeep, we drove past the grazing herds, stopped at an unmanned guard station and paused for photos of the riotous bougainvillea growing incongruously next to stacks of whitened elephant bones.

Best of all, we followed a track through huge thickets of towering trees and impenetrable thorny undergrowth: the jungle! Dean King would be proud of me!

Along the muddy track we saw teak trees with their light, mottled bark and big leaves. Pobby pointed out the cane plants, the material rattan furniture is made of, once weavers get past the long sharp thorns. The palm fronds grow six to eight feet high, taller in some places. The most fascinating were the silk cotton trees, enormous trees with multi-angled flanges coming off the trunk at the bottom, sort of like cypress knees. Pobby laughed when we took photos of each other next to one, trying to illustrate the scale.

Wild yams with big leaves grew in clumps on the ground while blooming bromeliads hung from host trees like Chinese lanterns at a party.

CENSUS REPORT OF K.N.P.

SPECIES	YEAR								
	1991	1993	1997	1999	2000	2006	2007	2008	2009
RHINO	1129	1164	-	1552	-	1855	-	-	2048
TIGER	-	72	80	-	86	-	-	-	-
SWAMP DEER	-	-	-	398	468	-	681	-	-
ELEPHANT	-	-	-	-	-	-	-	1293	-
WILD BUFFALO	-	-	-	1192	-	-	-	1937	-

Flying through the trees making raucous calls and sweet tweets were bright red and blue and gold birds. The brilliant blue Indian roller was easily identifiable as well as the kingfisher, a two-for-one bird with a tuxedo breast and an evening gown back of iridescent cerulean blue.

The jungle was a riot of wildlife, but you had to develop an eye to see it, so well camouflaged are most creatures, large and small. A mongoose scurried across our path. A monitor lizard crawled undisturbed over some rocks. A tiny lizard with a ruffled fan around his neck and an iridescent orange tail sat on the railing of a bamboo bridge.

We returned to Diphlu at noon. We were met at the reception hut as usual by the girls with hot towels and guava juice. Then Bo and I enjoyed tea on the verandah of our basha, thirty feet from the water's edge, and watched a man squatting in a narrow bamboo canoe paddling through the water hyacinths. Across the fifty-foot channel was a broad shoreline that is apparently inundated during the monsoons. Cattle and goats were grazing.

We had lunch of Chinese food, then more verandah time before heading back to the reception hut to meet the jeep for our afternoon safari.

Bo had seen a "rhino crossing" sign somewhere and I wanted a picture, but we couldn't find it. I had to settle for a "tiger crossing" sign.

Coming back from the park at lunch we got to see the neighborhood in daylight and twice we passed boys riding elephants down the highway, just like you'd pass George Taylor on his tractor at home.

We also passed a celebration of the Holi Festival, also called "colors" because of the pinky-purple powder everyone puts on his face. Holi was an evil goddess whom the minor gods demanded the major god kill, so he invited her into fire and she perished.

Despite the violent origin, Holi is a day of friendship. Ashook, who was our quoted authority on everything Indian, had told us about Holi. "If you have enemy, go have lunch or something to drink." People mark the day by spraying each other with colored powder. We drove by a place where young people were celebrating by trying to knock down a sort of piñata full of colored powder. The young men formed a circle and others got on their shoulders and still others climbed up to make a third level and hold one of their fellows up with a stick. The crowd staggered and swayed and fell down in the mud several times. The girls circled around cheering them on and line-dancing. Finally, one boy broke the piñata and colored dust blew all over the crowd. According to Ashook, somewhere in all this, girls pray to Vishnu for a husband and a nice house.

Having already committed to Shiva, Bo was not tempted to adopt Holi as his faith. However, the notion of having a god for everything was growing on me. We could see that Hinduism in all its cultural and theological manifestations was an integral part of everyday life for the majority of Indian citizens. Hinduism doesn't have a central text, like the Bible, nor does it have a central ecclesiastic hierarchy. There are many sects and branches, each with its own priorities regarding gods and related practices. Hindu tradition and practice have evolved in the past century, accommodating the civil outlawing of child marriages, the caste system and suttee, the self-immolation of widows.

The afternoon safari was lovely. We went to another lookout tower—this one overlooking a large lake or lagoon, gorgeous with the sun's rays stretching across the water in the late afternoon. We could see across the water elephants, water buffalo, rhino and deer. Egrets on the backs of the water buffalo and rhinos, cranes standing in the marsh, flocks of birds skimming the water, a solitary bird in bright plumage soaring close to our tower. It was an incredible sight, a picture of Nature without Man. We stayed a long time. When we started to leave, there was again some disturbance across the way and Pobby ran back up with his binoculars, looking for a big cat.

He was determined to show us a tiger, bless his heart.

At the end of the day as we headed out, another driver passed the information that the deer had sounded an alarm call, so safari jeeps stopped all around the perimeter of a large savannah and the guides all glued their eyes to binoculars.

But alas, no tiger. Just a lone elephant who looked majestic in his solitude.

Pobby said you have to stay three or four days to see a tiger.

I told him as much as I dreamed of seeing a tiger, I knew it was like winning the lottery, and that I had had the best time of my life all day today, thanks to him. It was enough for me to know that India actively promoted tiger conservation. He seemed grateful for my comments but I know he was disappointed. Most of the Indians we met throughout our trip were determined to give us the experience we wanted.

We continued to receive the VIP treatment at the lodge. When we came in from the afternoon jeep safari, the girls had tea for us on the bamboo bridge overlooking the rice paddy and lily pond in the middle of the compound. And the sun was shining.

We repaired to our verandah for cocktails. Bo had his gin and tonic, then he went for his shower with the illusion of privacy while I had my vodka and tonic and happily anticipated my own shower.

Rested and refreshed, we looked forward to Ledo tomorrow. The Holy Grail.

March 20, 2011
After dinner

Dinner was another delicious but solitary affair. The other guests had left. It was the end of the tourist season. The rain was beginning. We had drinks with Bijoy and an interesting conversation about Assamese politics. It all used to be Assam, but now there are seven states, plus a section of Darjeeling called Sikkim that has seceded. Locally they refer to the new smaller states as the seven sisters and one brother. There are elements throughout Assam that would like to secede altogether, causing unrest there and headaches in Delhi, 1,500 miles away. The region is connected to India proper by a narrow neck of land, barely fifteen miles wide in one place, so it's easy to understand the disconnect residents feel.

As usual, Robin the Reporter interviewed our companion. Bijoy is a tall, attractive, thirty-four-year-old man, very well-spoken with excellent English, the son of a tea plantation employee from Tinsukia.

He told us the tea plantations provide all services for employees—housing, some food ration, health care clinics and schools—sort of like the old coal mining companies in America used to do. It's a somewhat closed world. Bijoy said it was all he knew until he was twenty-five and decided to leave and do something else. When his father retired, the family moved to a house he had bought many years before in anticipation of retirement. Bijoy got interested in tourism and hospitality—evidently a growth industry in India—and studied hospitality management at Tezpur, just as Bud had.

We complimented Bijoy on his staff. Pobby showed up but not to have a drink. We showered praise on him in front of Bijoy.

Then we had dinner, complete with a printed menu. Something we had was made with "banana flower perpration in Assamese fashion".

The onion soup to start was good. It was all good but the onion soup was the only thing identifiable, except rice of course.

We talked about Dad and agreed he would love this place—and they would love him. I could hear him saying, "It's hell to get there, but once you do, it's first class." Dad was so profane.

Bo explained where the term "posh" came from: The British who travelled first class back and forth to India in colonial times always took cabins on the leeward side of the ship, thus "Port(side) Outgoing Starboard Homeward". P.O.S.H.

We had some dilemma about tipping. Prior to Diphlu we had gotten into the habit of Rs 500 for the guide and Rs 300 for the driver. (Given the skills of the drivers, we should have reversed the payments.) But at Diphlu we also tipped the bartender, tea lady servers and so forth. After dinner Bo tipped a few more people and gave some bills to the maître d' for the cook et al.

That left Bijoy. Bo thought because he had drinks with us and we socialized more or less as equals that it would be an insult to tip him. I could see his point, but the other side was that he had made sure we got the royal treatment. Maybe he didn't have anything else to do since we were the only guests, but anyway, it was very very nice. We truly enjoyed not only the wildlife but the pleasant interlude in what was physically a hard trip. So we wanted to express our gratitude to him in an appropriate fashion. If we were tipping generously everyone else in the establishment, I didn't want to see him left out.

Ultimately, we left an envelope with a note and two batches of bills. At this late date, I can't remember what we said or how much money we left, but we conveyed the information that we wanted to thank him, as well as provide money to tip anyone we may have overlooked, hint hint.

Despite the four a.m. start, the two nights and one full day at Diphlu provided a restful break in what was a brutal schedule. So much so that we were reluctant to leave. The next day would bring another tough day of travel, including an eight-hour drive from Kaziranga to Dibrugarh and on to Digboi, preparatory to the final assault on Ledo.

Ledo, the piece de resistance of the whole trip. While I hoped we could travel beyond Ledo far enough to get a peek at Burma, I sensed seeing Burma would be like seeing a tiger.

CHAPTER 9

ZIGGING AND ZAGGING ACROSS UPPER ASSAM

KAZARINGA TO DIGBOI AND BACK TO TINSUKIA

March 21, 2011

Leaving Kaziranga, we headed northeast, deeper into the largely rural and tribal region that once held a vast military presence from which the Allies launched a decisive campaign against the Japanese in Burma. The Ledo Road. We were there to explore history, but current events frequently intruded.

The local tribal rivalries were too complex for me to understand, but I was aware that Bo and I were heading into a region that saw periodic eruptions of violence from activists promoting the ascendancy of this group or that one. Train travel in the region was somewhat risky, as was travel by bus. Unbeknownst to us until we got there, tensions were heightened by the upcoming elections just a few weeks out. Heavily armed men in uniforms made a visible statement of the government's intention to quell any outbreaks. There was great concern that activists were infiltrating the region in the runup to the election, and as we were strangers in town, suspicion occasionally fell on us.

As usual, though, the absolute terror inspired by traffic on Indian roads outweighed all other concerns or fears.

We reluctantly waved goodbye to our personal Raj-on-the-river bungalow at 8:30 a.m. and left with our new driver and guide/ interpreter. My contact at helptourism.com had hired this team and had put together an ambitious schedule of touring and travel. Fortunately, Butch and Sundance had gotten some rest at Diphlu because the next three days proved to be grueling and full of even more unexpected cultural experiences.

Prashantho, our driver, looked to be forty-five or fifty and spoke no English but was clearly in charge. Sumitra, a recent graduate of hospitality school, acted as translator, guide and interpreter and worked hard to project professionalism. A petite young lady of about twenty, she was dressed in slacks with a bright red scarf tossed over her shoulder in a way that I futilely tried to copy. She rode up front with Prashantho and they spoke Hindi, I guess, or probably Bengali. Or maybe Assamese.

It was to be another hard day on the rough Indian roads. The eight-hour drive from Diphlu to Digboi contained the usual terrifying moments eliciting brave laughter from Bo and me—although a couple of times we were speechless. Prashantho proved to be the most aggressive driver we had yet to ride with. *Butch, what were you thinking?*

Prashantho had a pink squeaky toy hanging from the rearview mirror, and the more he lurched and charged through traffic, the more the toy would swing until it hit the windshield and squeaked. Maybe he drove so hard because he knew how far we had to go, or maybe it was just a feature of Indian drivers. In both urban and suburban areas, there were the usual obstacles in the road, for which Prashantho seldom wavered and never braked—including, or perhaps especially, for pedestrians. By then I was sprinkling Bonine on my food at every meal.

The crosswalk and child-playing signs we saw showed a person running. An official "x sprint" sign means traffic is dangerous, you should RUN across the street. There is no time wasted on political correctness, just a recognition of reality on the ground and the advice to act pragmatically.

The bike lane in Assam seemed to be the centerline and we could not understand why there weren't a dozen deaths every day.

Mom always had a thing about cyclists, complaining bitterly about their cavalier attitude as they cruised through traffic, endangering themselves and putting the onus on automobile drivers to avoid hitting them. Given the Rs. 40,000 price of hitting a bullock, we wondered what a bicyclist in India cost. Probably less than a chicken, we decided. We made many jokes about Mom and her attitude towards cyclists, an attitude we grew to share.

We careened along at 45 miles per hour (75 to 80 kilometers per hour) and honestly, 45 never felt so fast. Once we finally hit the open road, in relative terms, there were rumble bars or speed bumps in the middle of the highway. Sometimes a bunch of rocks. Another mystery of Indian life.

In a rural area, my diary notes, "There's an unusually large number of animals in the road today. Calf nursing while cow crossing the road."

We thought we had been hardened to traffic danger in India before, but Prashantho gave us the advanced class. We laughed and chuckled nervously about close calls, as when Prashantho didn't brake for an oncoming passing car in our lane. When the pink squeaky toy banged on the windshield, Bo said, "The Squeak-o-Meter has redlined."

As if life wasn't exciting enough, it began to rain. Hard. Prashantho didn't slow down. Miraculously, the road seemed less crowded. The pedestrians and bikes were mostly gone, leading me to think perhaps the safest time to drive was during a good rain.

Except of course the remaining bike riders were carrying umbrellas.

We were stopped a couple times by soldiers at check points. "Tour company with tourists…foreign nationals" was clearly what Sumitra and Prashantho told them. They cast a studiously dismissively glance our way and waved us on.

We had a tea break at 11 a.m. and lunch at 1:30 or 2:00 p.m., plus a bank stop somewhere. At the tea break place, there was a boy cleaning cages out front containing white rabbits and white rats. We presumed they were on the menu and tried to order something else.

The wash room was the depressingly familiar cell of filth, a level of quality that was maintained at our other stops throughout the day.

Bo and I had a system. He would go first and check things out—not that I had any choice in the end. At the tea break stop, he came back and said, "Use the one with the door." I thought, well, that's a new low.

North from Kaziranga to Dibrugarh, then east to Tinsukia, Digboi and Ledo.

After lunch, we reached Dibrugarh, a city of more than a million people and home to the airport we would depart from several days hence. At our request, Prashantho drove us to a commercial area where we hoped to find an internet café so I could email Cricket and let him know we were okay. I had not communicated with him since we were in Darjeeling. The café we found in Dibrugarh was a hole in the wall, a little warren of three or four cubicle-rooms with big old all-in-one units, the kind where the keyboard and the screen are built into one box. The computers were ancient boxes with dial-up connections. We paid a few rupees for ten-minute increments. It was amazing that the proprietor kept those machines running and maintained any connection to the telephone system at all. Service was so slow I kept having to buy more minutes, but I did pick up some emails from my anxious husband and I was able to send a message that we were fine, just finding it difficult to communicate with the outside world. We were fine, but we were a long damn way from civilization if something happened.

We also stopped at the Bank of India in Dibrugarh. We needed to get Rs 10,000 (about $215 at that time) to pay the tour operator—helptourism.com—for the Ledo Road part of the trip and Rs 3,000-4,000 ($65-86) to get us through our last few days in India.

The plan had been for Bo and me each to withdraw money and pool it as a kitty throughout the trip, but I was often unable to contribute because my debit card didn't work very well over there. Bo's worked fine. (I decided later I was using a credit card with the debit card PIN.) After the Bank of India ATM refused my card, we went inside where Bo withdrew Rs 10,000 and Rs 4,000 without a problem. I told Sumitra, "It's because he's a man," and she laughed and laughed. "We can't get equal rights," she said.

About 4:30 p.m. as we approached another urban area, Sumitra said brightly, "We have reached Digboi. What shall we be doing?"

You're asking me? Personally, I was ready for a drink and room service, but as it turned out, we were a loooong way from either one. I began to question whether Sumitra knew what the itinerary was.

I had found helptourism.com, our tour operator (and I use the term loosely), on the internet through Arif at amazingarunachal.com, which I found through IndiaMike.com. None of these outfits had been rated by Yelp or Trip Advisor. In addition to providing a driver and a guide and arranging the itinerary, helptourism.com connected me with Professor Hitendra Nath Sharma, the keeper of the flame of the Stilwell/Ledo Road. By email, Sharma agreed to tell us what he knew about the history of the area and perhaps show us around.

It was late in the booking process and I was thrilled to find someone who was promoting World War II heritage of the area, so I signed on, even though it seemed the proposed itinerary was a little ambitious from a time standpoint and the accommodations sounded more like Indian tourist lodges than Hyatt hotels.

(All part of the experience, I thought. And that was why I brought a man with me. I didn't know what the local experience involved.)

The itinerary called for us to tour the Digboi Oil Museum and meet with Professor Sharma after dinner, then spend the night at a lodge before driving as far out the Ledo Road the next day as the authorities would allow. This was to be followed by an overnight at the Dihing River Camp with a local-style feast and dancers in native dress. All well and good for the tourists, ignorant of the vast distances and poor roads ahead.

The ambitiousness of the itinerary made its frustrating appearance soon after our arrival in Digboi. At first, though, we found the usual anomalous sights.

We stopped at a railroad crossing with the engine off, waiting and watching the scenery. Digboi is a city, with city things like Rotary Clubs. We saw the familiar insignia on a sign: "Digboi is your town. Keep it clean. Rotary Club of Digboi." The sign post was surrounded by trash. All around us pedestrians and bikers crawled under the railroad gates and crossed the tracks. Amazingly, a short passenger train zipped through without killing anyone.

The Digboi Oil Museum is on the grounds of the Digboi Oil Refinery. When we reached the refinery at something well past 5 p.m., we found a sign that said, "Plying of Outside Vehicles Not Permitted." No entry into the refinery except company cars. In any event, the museum was closed, which was not a great loss because we had not traveled 10,000 miles on rough roads to see the oldest oil well in India.

As a suitable alternative, we went to the World War II cemetery maintained by the British Commonwealth War Memorial Commission. It is quite lovely, an archway with a bench facing the gravesites, a twenty-foot cross in the middle, and rows of gravestones with brass markers and flowers in between. The grass is clipped and edged to perfection. The flowers are groomed. There are maybe 250 graves there, nearly all Brits, but a handful of Indians, some Muslims and a few unknowns. The markers have the men's ages, mostly early twenties, one at twenty years old, a few mid-thirties. The markers list the name, unit and age and sometimes a line or two of memorial text. "A good husband who is deeply missed by his wife and daughter," or "He gave his all for his country when duty called." But the heart-breaking ones say things like, "Sadly missed by Mom, Dad and Sister Kate."

We signed the registry for visitors and decided it was a fitting way to begin our exploration of the remains of the enormous military complex that covered half the province of Assam in the 1930s and 1940s.

Then the day took a bad turn.

We had by then run out of time to meet with Professor Sharma. However, Sumitra got him on the phone, and he said to come to his school the next morning. We were relieved that we hadn't lost the opportunity to speak to him but worried that a visit in the morning would necessarily cut into our exploration time. At the moment, however, we were just tired and hungry from a hard day's travel and no dinner. When we got to the Tourist Lodge at Digboi, presumably our accommodation for the night, Bo and I stood around for a long time without checking in or knowing what was going on as Sumitra wandered off and discussed our reservations, the room rates, the score of the cricket match, whatever. Then without a word of explanation, we were herded back to the car and driven to another such place where we stood around without checking in or knowing what was going on.

Sumitra was a nice little girl but not very experienced. When things went wrong, she didn't know how to handle the customer. It seemed we had gotten bumped from our room by election officials. Everyone was obsessed about the election three weeks hence because (1) they only have one every five years and (2) there was a lot at stake for both separatists and nationalists.

Finally, I confronted Sumitra standing in front of Lodge #2, where she and Prashantho were trying to secure a room for us. We could see through an open door our prospective lodging—a simple room with twin beds, mismatched spreads, mosquito nets, no A/C, bathroom down the hall—which would have been fine, because we just wanted to lie down, or do anything except get back in the car.

I told her, "We have traveled half way around the world to meet Professor Sharma and see the Ledo Road, which is nowhere near here and tomorrow is our last day and you need to fix this." She conferred with Prashantho, who made a phone call.

The election officials had taken all the local rooms, so the plan became for us to drive back to Tinsukia, a city we had passed through after leaving Dibrugarh, and stay there. We had already missed seeing the Digboi Oil Museum (not that we cared, but it was on our all-inclusive tour package), and we were not going to see World War II historian Professor Sharma that night. Even more troubling, we would be backtracking, sleeping one hour further away from Ledo.

We were not happy, mostly because we had traveled many many miles, most of them in death-defying jaw-cracking herky-jerky sprints of dodg'em traffic at 55 mph, and having survived that, we feared our one-day visit to the Ledo Road would be snatched from us. I was deeply worried. Also tired. It was dark, we didn't have a place to stay and we hadn't had supper. We were hangry.

I also tried to explain to Sumitra that it was better for us as tourists to know what was happening and not be thinking all the time, What is going on?

I was reminded of the English couple at Kaziranga whom we passed sitting in a non-operational jeep as the day was fading. Two Indians had the hood up, working on something. Our driver stopped and seemed to say, What is the problem? Need help? The other men seemed to reply, Small problem, we'll have it fixed soon. We drove on and I was confident everything was okay. Yet when we all got back to the lodge and Bo spoke to the English couple, they said they had been very worried because the drivers didn't tell them what was going on.

Sumitra said, Don't worry, we'll go back to Tinsukia in twenty minutes (an hour, in reality, of course) to a confirmed hotel.

My heart sank. Yes, we needed a bed (and food and strong drink) but the clock was ticking on our schedule. How could we possibly backtrack to Tinsukia and still have time to explore Ledo the next day? I told her firmly that we had come to see the Ledo Road, we didn't care about the Oil Museum or native tribal dancing, that the number one thing was seeing the Ledo Road, and we wanted to make sure we had all the time we needed for that. I was starting to get sick to my stomach. All this effort to get to Assam and see the remains of the Ledo Road and we had no control over traveling the last few miles to our goal. We didn't even know how few—or many—miles were left. We didn't know how to reach our prime resource, Professor Sharma, on our own. We were at the mercy of a blithe child who had just graduated from hospitality school and a maniac driver who didn't speak English.

But I had clearly gotten Sumitra's attention. She was already worried we'd be upset and now she was chastened. As the mature one on the team, Prashantho helped her a lot, telling her what to say.

There was nothing to do but return to Tinsukia, a wild drive in the dark in the rain on slick roads while Sumitra and Prashantho laughed and joked in Assamese and Butch and Sundance muttered darkly in the back. *Butch, what were you thinking?*

Regardless, we were pleased to see the Ballerina Hotel, a local independent institution but a major upgrade from the lodge. We would have been pleased to see a pallet with mosquito netting at that point. Shishira, helptourism.com's man in Tinsukia, greeted us at the hotel when we got there about 9 p.m. Later we saw him in the dining room. Bo said, "This place must be all right if this is where he hangs out."

The Hotel Ballerina in Tinsukia is probably as good as it gets for an independent Indian hotel. The room and bath were clean, if somewhat dingy. The bedroom was large and basic, although it had a mini-fridge and a small flat screen TV. Ensuite bathroom. They made up the couch into a bed, which Bo gallantly took. I assured him there was no difference between the couch-bed and the real bed or even the floor.

Although we had been planning to ask for an adjustment in the price (we hadn't paid anything yet for this leg), we decided to wait and see. It was close to 10 p.m. and we had not eaten anything since early afternoon, but fortunately the Ballerina Hotel had a restaurant—a normal indoor restaurant, not a café open to the mosquitoes and heat. We ordered some food and watched more of the mysterious cricket tournament on TV, drinking Fosters beer and laughing rather hysterically. Finally, we clinked glasses. "Here's to Bolivia!"

Tomorrow, the Ledo Road!

LEDO

Chapter 10

Walking on the Ledo Road

Ledo and Dihing River Camp

March 22, 2011

When our big day finally arrived, we did not know what to expect. That had been the case for most of the trip, in fact. We were open to seeing whatever there was to see, but that did not mean we were entirely prepared for the day's events, which were to be by turns, hair-raising, touching, hilarious and trying. Sort of like the whole trip, only more so.

A chastened Prashantho and Sumitra stood outside the Ballerina Hotel at 8 a.m., waiting to carry us to Ledo. For some reason, they were absolutely determined for us to see the Oil Museum at Digboi, to the point that they had arranged for us to be admitted before the normal opening hour. It was interesting, but my curiosity was compromised by anxiety over the fact that this was Not The Ledo Road.

Still, proving the wisdom of Dean King's insistence to *go there*, we picked up a few interesting factoids that enhanced my understanding of the enormous logistical effort the campaign to retake North Burma entailed.

We learned that Digboi was the home of India's first commercial oil well, the Discovery Well, established in 1889. Digboi was the home of vital oil resources for the Burma campaign. Later we passed huge open-pit coal mines. (And here I thought all they produced in Assam was tea.) This trove of local energy sources provided one of the few benefits to the staging area for building the Ledo Road, which was otherwise at the end of a long, tenuous supply chain. It also explained why the resource-poor Japanese were so eager to capture the area.

In addition to the road itself, U.S. forces constructed three pipelines parallel to The Road. These were built to transport motor gasoline, aviation fuel and diesel fuel from Ledo to Kunming, a distance of 928 miles. Many pumping stations were also built to keep the products flowing.

As we learned, the pipelines are defunct. The museum contains sections of six-inch pipe, once buried deep in the earth, retrieved from the jungle near Ledo. Little did we know as we gazed at the rusted scraps of metal but our tour of the historical remnants of World War II in Assam could be pretty well summed up in that display case. Like snow leopards, one-horned rhinos and Bengal tigers, traces of the war are elusive and dwindling.

Although I was worried that we wouldn't leave Digboi until noon and we wouldn't have enough time to meet with Professor Sharma and still get to Ledo, Sumitra and Prashantho insisted it would be ok. Given our experience with Indian concepts of time, we were not optimistic. We had no choice but to hope for the best. We finally got on the road to Margherita, where Professor Sharma presided over a private school.

When we arrived at Axom Junior College, we found a one-story building tucked under hollong trees and surrounded by bushes with long spiky fronds. In the lobby was a figure of Saraswati, the god of knowledge, holding books in one hand and a musical instrument in the other. The good professor wasn't immediately available, so we sat and waited about ten minutes. Someone brought us tea, the wonderful Indian tea served thick with milk and sugar.

Eventually Professor Sharma invited us into his office and we chatted a bit. He is a sprightly man with tufts of grey hair and a decided twinkle in his eye. Ever the curious reporter, I began to

pepper him with questions, first about his school and then about the area, past and present. Many schools in India seem to be privately owned. The equivalent of an American high school, Axon Junior College had opened the year before and at that time boasted fifty-two students in three grades. The curriculum included the humanities, English, Hindi, Assamese and math. The school has clearly flourished, with a recent Facebook page photo showing a student body of well over a hundred boys and girls.

As I jotted notes on a pad, the professor became visibly concerned, halted the interrogation and said, "Who are you? Why are you wanting to know these things?"

With the memory of gun-toting guards and roving election officials fresh in our minds, we immediately recognized his concerns and our error in being so inquisitive. We backtracked and explained our eagerness to see where our father had worked sixty-seven years earlier and our mission to walk the Ledo Road.

Eventually, he was persuaded that we were not government spies or anyone out to get him.

Relieved, he then got into a lively conversation with Bo as I continued to take notes. He recalled entertaining another man who was following his father's footsteps through Assam. Ron Blicker or Bleeker had left him a CD with the father's diary from the war. Sharma directed us to the Library of Congress to find the American soldier's diary.

Sharma began reciting statistics about the Ledo Road, which he and other locals refer to as the Stilwell Road, information that I either had or could readily obtain. I wasn't sure the visit was going to be very helpful and, anxious to get to Ledo, I was thinking about a graceful exit when he said, "I have to be back here by 2:30 but I'll go with you and show you everything."

That put a new spin on things. An informed local guide!

First, he said, "Will you be speaking to my class?"

When we entered the classroom, the students all stood up. There were eight to ten girls lined up by twos on the left side and about thirty-five to forty boys on the right.

Professor Sharma consulted his notes and called on me first, to my surprise. I got up and said it was an honor to be there, what we were doing, how Dad told us about India and we wanted to come see for ourselves, and praised the beauty of Assam—then turned it over to Bo. He said most of the same, adding that Dad said the Indian soldiers were brave, good soldiers and had sacrificed a lot.

Then we hit the road. Professor Sharma has a good sense of humor. We talked about the opening of the Ledo Road: On January 12, 1945, the first convoy left Ledo to travel the completed road to Kunming, China. Professor Sharma told us he remembered being at the celebration in Kunming. "I was there with my parents—very exciting day. I was four years old but I remember."

We were impressed but privately Bo wondered how he, an Indian, came to be in China that day, and I wondered whether the age calculation was right—if so, he'd be only four years older than Bo and he looked older than that.

Later when Bo asked him about it, he laughed and said he was joshing us.

He rode in front and would tap Prashantho's leg and direct him to turn down some little road or another where he would show us a slab of concrete overgrown with weeds and houses and say, Here's the roof of a big bunker, or Here's a part of the Stilwell Road. Gradually, by gesture and animated commentary, he answered our questions.

What is remaining from World War II to see?

Has much of the jungle been cleared or was it always open land here?

Did the British have a military camp in the area in the 1930s—before the war?

"On 16 December 1942, work started from Ledo on the road," Professor Sharma recited. "After six miles, they find they are building in the opposite direction. The Stilwell Road is still there. People use it in Burma still: the Kachins [a tribal people whose territory spans the border]. The road is good, the bridges have fallen. There is a plan to restore the bridges. We do believe it will be open again in three or four years."

After what we had seen in India, I was skeptical.

While I was thrilled to have a knowledgeable guide in the car, I was dismayed when he first directed Prashantho to drive back into Digboi, away from Ledo. *Will we never get there?*

At Digboi, we climbed down an overgrown bank to look at the entrance to a bunker. Nearby we saw gun emplacements for the anti-aircraft guns that were brought from Karachi to protect the refinery. That's probably two thousand miles of hard road. Imagine moving them so far, even by rail. Another indication of the massive logistics involved with fighting a war.

Before the war, there was no military camp in this area. From Digboi east to Jairampur and west to Dibrugarh, British private interests in the name of the Assam Railway and Trading Co.—AR&T—claimed the local resources of oil, gold, coal, timber and undeveloped land. The dense jungle was cleared for huge tea plantations in the nineteenth century, many centered around the town of Margherita, about ten miles from Digboi and the last significant town before reaching the Burmese border. In addition to being rich in natural resources, Assam has more than a thousand tea gardens, which together produce more than half the tea in India, some 700 million kilograms per year.

And indeed, much of the land appeared to be in cultivation with tea plants, interspersed with clumps of thick, jungle-like underbrush with tall stands of hollong trees shooting up out of the middle. Hollong trees reach 150 feet and are without branches except for a canopy at the top, making the trunks easy to process into plywood. Plywood is big business here, and not surprisingly, the hollong is the state tree of Assam.

The Margherita Tea Estate is the oldest one in the area, encompassing vast acreage on both sides of the Dihing River, a tributary of the Brahmaputra. We could see the backs of bullocks among the bushes in the tea gardens, just like the backs of rhinos in the elephant grass at Kaziranga. Out in the middle of a sweeping vista of tea bushes, we saw an attractive square bamboo house with a wrap-around porch and thatched roof, built on pillars and shaded by a few hollong trees. Home of the overseer?

Interestingly, in the past few years, the Modi administration has made a concerted effort to develop "tea tourism" in Assam, and various tea plantations have begun catering to tourists, much as the wineries do in the U.S. and elsewhere. There are reportedly some beautiful golf courses built during the Raj that are an additional focus of this tourism effort. Needless to say, such luxurious tourism was not available to Butch and Sundance in 2011—and would not have been on our itinerary if it had.

In those pre-tourism days, as we drove through Margherita, we were more focused on the railroad tracks running alongside the road and the tea bushes growing up to the edge of the tracks. In the distance, miles of open pit coal mines pocked the hills. Here, far from urban areas, the smog was gone, but coal dust hung in the air. Margherita is known locally as "Coal Queen."

Rolling through town, we passed a sign: "If married, divorce speed." Does that mean fast or slow? Prashantho was driving with relative moderation, prepared to stop and turn at the professor's request, but there was nothing of wartime interest here.

However, as we drove through the next village beyond Margherita, Bo and I realized with a shock…this was Ledo!

Ledo had taken an almost mythic hold on our imaginations since we first heard Dad speak of it in our childhood, and we eagerly drank in the view. At last, after thousands of air miles and hundreds of rough road miles, after scores of Bonine tablets, we had reached that remote spot in the far back of beyond, once the center of the Allied war effort in the China-Burma-India theater of war—Ledo!

Ledo is a small town of about 15,000 people, the railhead for the Assam-Bengal Railway, the spot through which all the supplies for building the Ledo Road passed. All the equipment, all the laborers, all the soldiers who cleared the jungle of Japanese ahead of the construction, everything and everyone passed through Ledo, either by train or by plane or by shank's mare. We looked at the village in wonder, trying to imagine the activity that filled the streets nearly seventy years earlier. Once there were 20,000 workers encamped near Ledo. Professor Sharma says they spoke 200 languages.

But the hustle and bustle of the 1940s is gone. The unpainted train station is tired and filthy, the roads are quiet and dusty. The buildings are monochromatic. It reminded me of an American town in the West after the silver mines played out. Tellingly, the street sign proclaiming "LEDO" was surrounded by a huge mound of garbage.

The excitement Bo and I felt upon reaching Ledo—Ledo!—was immediately dashed.

Jeesh, all Bolivia can't look like this.

How do you know? This might be the garden spot of the whole country. People may travel hundreds of miles just to get to this spot.

We had traveled a long hard road to get to this place and, garden spot or not, we wanted proof that we had been to Ledo.

Professor Sharma and Prashantho were chatting in Assamese and it was clear our World War II guide had nothing to show us here. But Ledo and Pangsau Pass were the geographic targets of this adventurous journey. We wanted to memorialize our visit here. Without the prospect of buying a t-shirt—"I walked the Ledo Road"—we asked Prashantho to stop so Sumitra could take a picture of Bo and me in front of the sign saying "Ledo." We have two photos, one close-up of our head and shoulders underneath the sign. The other is a full-length photo showing us standing on the mound of garbage surrounding the sign.

Aside from that photo opportunity, we didn't stop in Ledo. I don't know what I expected, but the scene was deeply anticlimactic. I had always conjured visions of the teeming military industrial complex that swept across upper Assam, and I thought there would at least be old military signs and repurposed corrugated sheds and rows of bamboo *bashas*. But so far, nothing to indicate this was once the launchpad of a major wartime campaign.

A mile or so further, we turned off the highway and drove down a dirt road through two concrete obelisks. Professor Sharma made the electrifying announcement that the broad open space before us was the Ledo airstrip. At last! *All right, Dean King, we are here.*

But even this place was underwhelming. The site where ten thousand flights took off in the urgency of war presented a pastoral image. Two runways were still visible and the surrounding land was open, undeveloped, uncultivated. A few cows grazed the grass growing in the concrete cracks and a boy rode a bike. They use the site for an annual festival, Sharma told us.

Prashantho drove to the end of the runway. There Bo and I got out and gazed down the broken weedy concrete slab and communed with history, trying to hear the drone of DC-3s touching down with a load of raw Chinese recruits to be trained and lumbering away with a load of supplies for Kunming, five hundred miles over the Himalayas. Fifteen hundred flights ended in death on the side of the snowy peaks. Some planes leaving from the spot where we stood flew over the Burmese jungle and dropped supplies that Dad had ordered for his unit, the 66th Chinese Regiment. For the first time in our nerve-wracking, culture-shocking, hilarious, adventurous dash across the subcontinent of India, we paused and felt the ghost of Major Traywick, a twenty-four-year-old American Army officer living his own personal adventure amidst the chaos, confusion, danger, and absurdities of global war. He was here, in this very spot.

We returned to our car at once sobered and satisfied that we were touching history. As we settled in, Bo and I grinned at each

other. This was what we had come for. Suddenly, at the professor's behest, Prashantho floored the gas and we hurtled down the runway in the car. Sharma called out, "Last flight off Ledo airstrip!" and cackled with laughter.

It was one of those moments that filled me with love for India and her people.

From the airstrip we drove a few miles to the Ledo Club, formerly the Allied Officers Club, now an active gathering place for Indian officials. During the war, Admiral Louis Mountbatten stayed in a bungalow there. We got out and walked around, admiring the flowers and wondering if Dad stayed there—*probably not*—or had a drink there—*could have*. The foundation of the BOQ—Bachelor Officers' Quarters—was still there, a rectangle of concrete.

After so many hours in the car together, we had become quite chummy and we took lots of pictures of each other, except for Prashantho, who somehow avoided the camera. I admired the way Sumitra wore her bright red scarf but when I tried to wear mine the same way, it wouldn't stay in place, so she showed me how to pin it on. "Oh! You pin it!"

Beyond Ledo, the land was flat with a few hills to the south. Just east of Ledo, we came to Stilwell Park, a small pullover with a billboard map showing where the Ledo Road goes. This, Professor Sharma informed us proudly, was the beginning of The Road, called the Stilwell Road by locals. Again, we experienced conflicting emotions. Undeniably, Bo and I felt elated, walking on more ground hallowed by our father's footsteps, while our companions basked in our excitement.

Yet we couldn't help but feel a bit wistful. For all its exotic and bloody history, the site held none of the gravity of other World War II commemorative sites. Think of the historic trail of professional markers and immaculately-groomed cemeteries along the coast of Normandy. Here, the billboard immortalizing the Ledo-Stilwell-Burma Road was hand-painted. The scrap of road

running beneath the billboard was cracked by weeds shouldering their way through. The tiny memorial garden held two blue concrete benches growing lichens and shaded by green canopies of corrugated tin scavenged from wartime hangars or barracks. White paint was peeling from the wrought iron fence enclosing the park.

In Normandy, with all its solemn monuments and rows of crosses visited each year by hundreds of thousands of people, the theme is Never Forget. In Assam, the war has long been forgotten. In China, 900 miles away at the other end of the Road, there are markers and memorials honoring those who worked on the road, the soldiers who fought the Japanese in North Burma and the airmen who flew the Hump from Assam to Yunnan.

But in Assam, in northeast India, all that exists to commemorate the hundreds of thousands of people who camped here and left here to work-fight-die in the massive China-Burma-India theater of war is Stilwell Park, a crude poster and an untended garden catching the eye of passing motorists and the rare pilgrim following her father's footsteps.

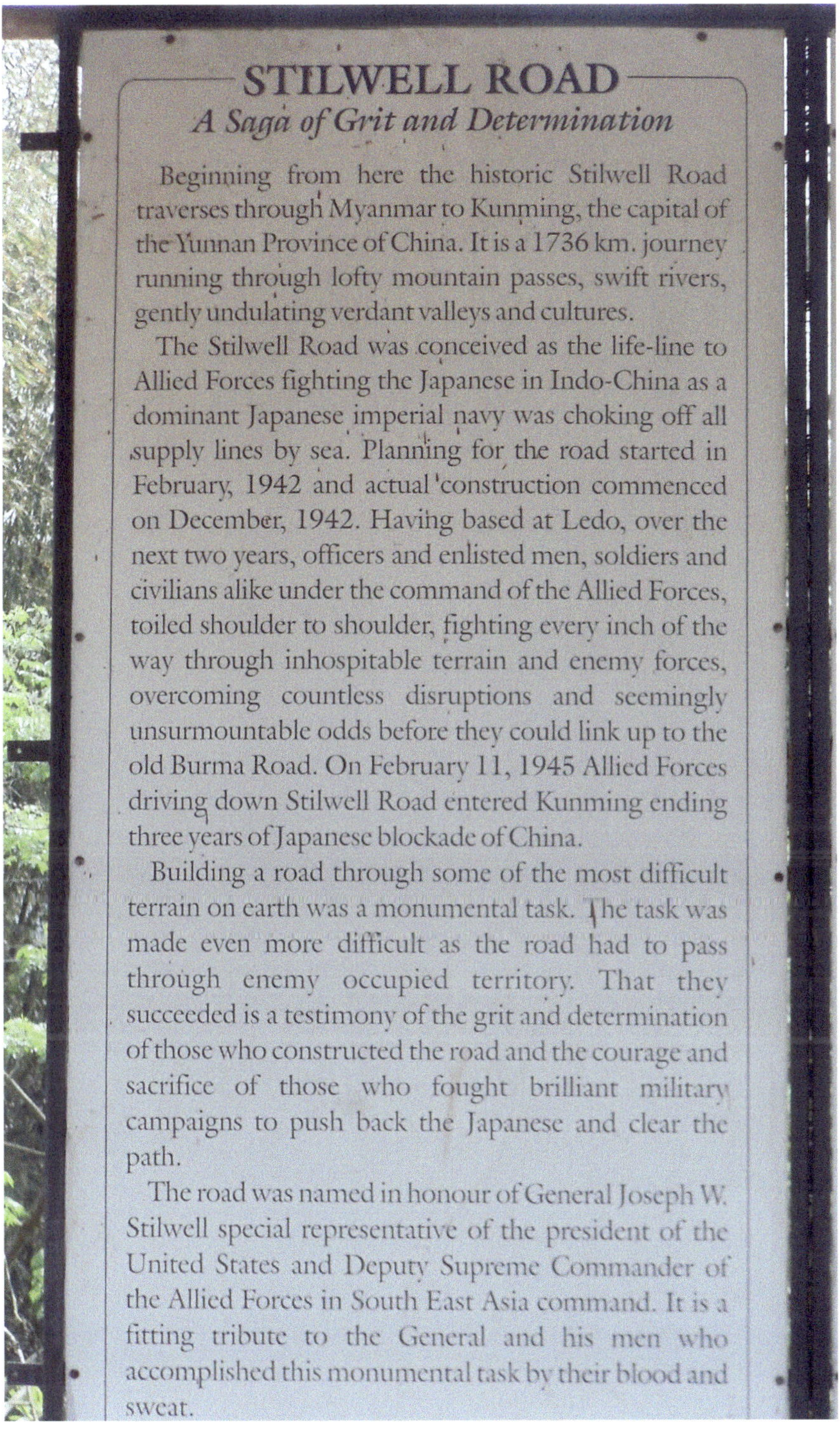

STILWELL ROAD

A Saga of Grit and Determination

Beginning from here the historic Stilwell Road traverses through Myanmar to Kunming, the capital of the Yunnan Province of China. It is a 1736 km. journey running through lofty mountain passes, swift rivers, gently undulating verdant valleys and cultures.

The Stilwell Road was conceived as the life-line to Allied Forces fighting the Japanese in Indo-China as a dominant Japanese imperial navy was choking off all supply lines by sea. Planning for the road started in February, 1942 and actual construction commenced on December, 1942. Having based at Ledo, over the next two years, officers and enlisted men, soldiers and civilians alike under the command of the Allied Forces, toiled shoulder to shoulder, fighting every inch of the way through inhospitable terrain and enemy forces, overcoming countless disruptions and seemingly unsurmountable odds before they could link up to the old Burma Road. On February 11, 1945 Allied Forces driving down Stilwell Road entered Kunming ending three years of Japanese blockade of China.

Building a road through some of the most difficult terrain on earth was a monumental task. The task was made even more difficult as the road had to pass through enemy occupied territory. That they succeeded is a testimony of the grit and determination of those who constructed the road and the courage and sacrifice of those who fought brilliant military campaigns to push back the Japanese and clear the path.

The road was named in honour of General Joseph W. Stilwell special representative of the president of the United States and Deputy Supreme Commander of the Allied Forces in South East Asia command. It is a fitting tribute to the General and his men who accomplished this monumental task by their blood and sweat.

As we left Stilwell Park and continued north on Highway 315, a new road built on top of the Ledo/Stilwell Road, I kept thinking about how this whole area had been teak jungle and hollong groves, cleared for tea in the 19th century and then for the military complex in the 1940s. Astonishingly, there was virtually nothing left to indicate this was once a huge military base, stretching all the way back to Dibrugarh. Much of the area has been reclaimed for growing the world-famous Assam tea. (Unfortunately, deforestation for tea farms and plantations is causing another war by bringing the region's 5,700 wild elephants into increasing conflict with the human population, resulting in dozens of deaths for both man and beast every year.)

At Lekhapani, the usual pot holes took over the road, stretches of which were made of cobblestone. Sharma pointed out the remains of the Lekhapani air strip, a scrap of rocky surface on the grounds of a school. Straight ahead, to the north, we could see the lower Himalayas in the distance. To the right, to the east, we could see hills, beyond which lay the Patkai Mountains and the famed Pangsau Pass where the Ledo Road crosses into Burma. Our excitement was building again. Would we make it to the Burmese border?

At Longtong, we crossed a buff-colored concrete bridge over the Dihing River. One of several such that we saw, the bridge was sturdy and straight, bearing the design characteristics of military construction. A relic of the war? Or older British occupation? The water was so low that we could see people down in the wide river bed, washing clothes in the stream and grazing animals.

According to Sharma, a Gurkha regiment of Nepalese soldiers settled here after the war, which got me thinking about how war ends up moving people around, spreading cultures and impacting local populations.

Further on, we stopped by the side of the road and walked around a large cemetery of Chinese graves. The field had a low wall. Even so, there was a calf grazing among the stones. Many

were turned over. Having seen the crisply maintained British Commonwealth Cemetery at Digboi, it made me sad to see these Chinese graves had been virtually abandoned. Somewhere in China there are families who don't know where their loved ones lie. Dad's ghost appeared here, too, as the cemetery undoubtedly held the remains of men from his unit.

After training Chinese troops in Ramgarh, India, in 1943, Dad and his assigned regiment moved to Ledo to prepare for the reconquest of Burma. Dad said he lived in a bamboo *basha* at Milepost 14 on the Ledo Road. He had several adventures in the three months that he lived there: nearly getting killed by a runaway pack horse and being threatened by a pistol-toting drunk lieutenant after a night of revelry together.

Today, Milepost 14 is marked approximately by the village of Jagun. We could not identify any of the bamboo structures as possible leftovers from Dad's era, but there were other remnants of the war. We pulled into a driveway and walked on a slab of metal that Sharma said covered a huge underground bunker. Now there are four houses on top of it. He said the Japanese came close enough to bomb this area—possibly explaining how Dad's *basha* burned up with all his belongings while he was in the jungle. Jagun is probably only fifteen miles from Burma as the crow flies. The highway turns sharply towards Burma there and we could see the Patkai Mountains, ribs jutting south at the end of the Himalayas.

Out in the country on Highway 315, Prashantho reached speeds of 90 kph (55 mph). Twelve kilometers from Jairampur, the land becomes hilly. Jairampur is a guarded border crossing into Arunachal Pradesh, which borders both Burma and China. Assam has been divided into seven smaller states since Dad was here, of which Arunachal Pradesh is one. It is very tribal, we were told. At the time, serious domestic unrest coupled with simmering border disputes with China led the government to restrict access to the state. My dream of reaching Pangsau Pass involved passage through Jairampur to Arunachal Pradesh, which required a permit, which I had been unable to obtain.

Jairampur is where author Donovan Webster, in the introduction to my favorite book, *The Burma Road*, meets "Sunglasses" and is turned back from hiking closer to Burma despite an attempted bribe of cigarettes. Thanks to Professor

Sharma, we didn't have too much trouble in Jairampur, but things got very hairy beyond there.

At Jairampur there was a gate with armed, uniformed guards. The road is on a sort of causeway, with a steep hillside down to an area with cows. Prashantho stopped at the gate and the guards approached. "May I know your identities?" One guard took our passports while the other lingered by the car.

Bo hissed at me not to take any photographs, while Professor Sharma explained that our father had lived there during the war. After awhile they waved us through. I couldn't wait to tell Donovan we got through Jairampur!

On the other side of town at the Assam Rifles gate, we slowed down but no one stopped us. Professor Sharma pointed to the mountains just in front of us, drawing our attention to a particular notch. "Pangsau Pass." We were salivating. I'd seen many pictures of the switchback road leading up to the pass and many pictures of soldiers and trucks and jeeps crossing the pass with the hand-painted sign hammered into the dirt: *Pangsau Pass 3727 feet*. Known as Hell Gate, the pass marked the gateway to Burma for tens of thousands of soldiers and road builders in the 1940s. Today, through the tourism efforts of AmazingArunachalPradesh.com, there are several tribal festivals in the area, including the Pangsau Pass Festival at Nampong. There are several cemeteries along the road, according to Professor Sharma, some holding American graves. As I write in 2023, the U. S. government has initiated a dialogue with officials in Assam in a belated search for the remains of American soldiers. While I'd like to think this means officials will at last put up a fitting memorial to the conflict of the 1940s, the region is riven by a new conflict, potentially quite serious, as China boldly claims Arunachal Pradesh for itself.

As we rolled along towards Nampong and the final five or ten miles to the pass, we reached a third gate. Here, the guards were on full alert. Professor Sharma pleaded with them to let us go just a little ways to see the World War II cemetery because our father was there during the war yadda yadda. "These are Americans. They are wanting to see where their father lived." No deal. We were sternly turned back.

Then, when we backtracked to the second gate (Assam Rifles), which we had previously sailed through without being stopped, the guards rushed out to accost us with extremely warlike weapons. They asked many questions in Assamese, which Sharma answered in his soothing and authoritative manner. We were in the dark of course, anxious and worried. Then they took our passports and went into their building, which was much more solid and official-looking than the hut at Jairampur. Again, Bo hissed at me not to take any photographs as we sweated in the back seat, trying to look invisible. *Butch, what were you thinking?*

I was thinking, *We get out of here alive, we go to Australia. Goodbye, Bolivia. Hello, Australia.*

It was a very sobering experience. I for one spent most of it worrying that Cricket would never know what happened to us. As we anxiously waited, Professor Sharma explained to us regarding our first pass through the gate, "Things are going slow in India, and when they are not coming out, I thought it was okay."

It was more evidence of the nervousness over the upcoming regional elections. We had seen that in Professor Sharma's own suspicion of us as we sat in his office taking notes. Additionally, we recalled the governor's visit to Darjeeling that rerouted our departure, the confiscation by election officials of our rooms at the tourist lodge in Digboi and the frequent stops by armed troops as we drove through Dibrugarh, Tinsukia and Digboi. Maybe the officials had tracked us across Assam and decided we were in fact undercover activists bent on disrupting the election in favor of some violent tribal faction. Or maybe we just picked a dicey time to go to Assam. (At least we had dropped Cairo from our itinerary, Cairo, which was then in flames at the launch of the Arab Spring.)

Eventually, with little ceremony, the guard returned the passports and let us go. I'm sure the elections made the situation more ticklish than it would have been ordinarily, but I couldn't relax until hours later when we regained the comforting familiarity of barreling down the highway dodging auto-rickshaws and sleeping cattle while Prashantho's squeaky toy bounced off the windshield.

Before dropping Professor Sharma at his school, we stopped for lunch at a lovely restaurant. Rice wrapped in a huge leaf, shish kebab, dal, noodles in gravy. When the food appeared, Professor Sharma said, "Let us wait. Let us wait for spoons to come."

There was a moment of awkwardness towards the end of the meal when I had not cleaned my plate. Even though we were paying for the meal, it was expected that we would eat every crumb on our plates. It is a country of starving people, after all.

We were periodically concerned about the large portions of food we were served at various places. Sumitra and the locals carefully ate every grain of rice on their plates, but they loaded us up with food of so many kinds that often I could not finish it all.

At lunch with Professor Sharma, he noted my plate, which held a generous amount of rice and a few bites of other food, and said, "You love the animals, eh?"

"Will the animals get this?" I asked.

When he nodded, I smiled and said, "I love animals very much."

That lunch was one of the best meals we had in India and the restaurant was one of the nicest. I wanted to take advantage of the facilities in a place that looked neater than any restaurant so far, but Sumitra came back and said, No, too dirty. That was a stunning comment, I thought, having seen places that I thought could not possibly be more filthy and unsanitary. (Later she asked if I wanted to stop at a gas station—yes—the restroom was kept locked! And it was pretty clean.)

After lunch, we bid farewell to Professor Sharma, thanking him profusely and exchanging email addresses. His charm and his knowledge of the area were indispensable to our exploration. Since there are so few traces of the military-industrial complex remaining, we would have seen nothing but tea plantations and hollong trees without Sharma. While I had vaguely anticipated seeing perhaps a Quonset hut converted to tea storage or remains of the 20th General Hospital, I wasn't disappointed as much as stunned that such a vast military-industrial complex could simply vanish.

As we drove west on the next mysterious leg of the trip, I couldn't help but think, *Where did it all go?* When I could tear my eyes away from watching the road through the windshield, I watched the passing scenery. Millions of Indians live within a hundred yards of the highway, taking shelter in rude tents and actual holes covered by makeshift lean-tos constructed out of pieces of corrugated metal. Finally, it dawned on me: *There* are the remains of the temporary sheds and offices and barracks. Piece by piece they have been repurposed as shelter for the homeless millions in India.

Talk about turning swords into plowshares.

I had plenty of time to mull over what we had seen and not seen, the fright the gun-toting officials gave us, the charming conversation with Professor Sharma, because we were back to three-plus hours of hard driving with Prashantho. By then I was tossing down Bonine like popcorn. Although we did not know it, Prashantho and Sumitra were taking us *beyond* Dibrugarh to spend the night at Dihing River Camp—one hundred and fifty kilometers, more than three and a half hours away. By the time we reached the camp entrance, bouncing through mud holes deep enough to swallow a small car, we had traveled more than three hundred kilometers—about two hundred miles—that day. This on top of a four hundred km (265 miles) day the day before.

When we got as far as Tinsukia, around 4 p.m., every truck in India was there. We sat in a roundabout in a traffic jam worthy of I-95. A uniformed man on top of the stone edifice in the center of the intersection waved his arms and blew his whistle in an attempt to direct traffic. As we watched, he suddenly stopped, pocketed his whistle, got down off the stone circle, waded through the traffic to the sidewalk and disappeared. Shift over.

Dihing River Camp was really a camp, as in no electricity. It was a commercial enterprise of Prashantho and some partners to promote (and benefit from) eco-tourism. Indians are very entrepreneurial. The camp was built on the river, which had sheer banks of at least ten feet. The access road was a wide muddy track running along the bank, cut with deep ruts and deeper pits full of soupy mud. It was dusk when we arrived, so we didn't get the full effect until the next morning.

Dihing River Camp had four main buildings in a picket-fenced compound, all very new, all *basha*-style bamboo walls and

decks with thatched roofs. They were furnished with a couple of chairs and some kind of pallet on the floor with sheets and a pillow and two of the heaviest—as in densest—blankets I've ever seen. They gave us faux lanterns that ran on batteries. Plus, Bo and I had our own small flashlights that we had brought with us.

Nearby was a two-room bathhouse. We were assigned one room/side, which held a shower head and drain, a western toilet—with paper!—and a basin. All cold water of course, but running, thanks to gravity and the ubiquitous black casks of water mounted on a platform.

In addition to two *bashas* for guests and a long kitchen/staff bunkhouse, the camp had a pavilion with a thatched roof and concrete floor, maybe twenty by forty feet. This was the dining and entertainment room. All the buildings and the concrete walkways were surrounded by carefully maintained beds of flowering plants: Coleus and vinca grow on woody bushes here, not as annuals only.

We arrived at dusk, maybe eight p.m., and we were starving, so we were glad to have a big dinner. The food was well prepared, nicely served and delicious—and abundant! As usual, we did not recognize most of it, but that did not affect our appreciation of a good meal. Prashantho's outfit had prepared not only a feast but a lengthy entertainment program involving a dozen men and women, including two young girls, all dressed in elaborate native costumes and performing a variety of dances. They had a boom box for most of the program, but a few of the men played instruments, as well. Even with sustenance, we were pretty tired, but we stayed and clapped through the long, repetitive performance, even joining in the dances at the end, and of course heaping praise and gratitude on everybody.

We were so tired we could hardly process the events of the day—actually setting foot in the near-mythic village of Ledo, viewing the rather astonishing lack of remains from the huge military complex of the 1940s and now falling asleep in a bamboo hut on the banks of the Dihing River. But we managed to appreciate the fact we were sleeping in a *basha* on the eve of Dad's birthday.

Good night, Butch.

Good night, Sundance.

Chapter 11

Back to Civilization -- Kolkata

March 23, 2011
Dad's 93d birthday

After a late night of revelry at the Dihing River Camp, we had to have an early breakfast and make the usual hard drive somewhere, this time to the airport at Dibrugarh for a midday flight. We could barely see the road into the camp in the dusk when we had arrived, but oh boy when we left…

The road ran alongside the Dihing River with no shoulder and no guard rail. Although the road was wide, it was slick red clay and contained ruts—mud-bogging holes—full of soupy mud deep enough to swallow a small car. Prashantho's strategy for getting through depended heavily on momentum. He drove as fast as possible, trying to swerve around the worst of the mud holes but occasionally dropping a wheel in one. This tactic resulted in the car fishtailing and spinning crazily, skidding out of control close to the riverbank—a ten-foot drop into the water. Since my greatest fear in life is to be trapped underwater in a car, I experienced a high level of anxiety.

When we got ready to leave that morning, Bo discovered that Prashantho's Land Rover-lookalike was only 2-wheel drive. He was afraid we'd get stuck in a mud hole and miss our flight, and I was afraid we'd shoot off the bank into the river and die. To improve our chances for getting back to the highway, Bo insisted that Prashantho round up all the men at the Dihing River Camp and have them hang onto the top and back of the car to weigh it down and provide more traction. It worked and we got out, but not until we had a couple of close calls. Characteristically, the locals all laughed about how much fun we were having.

We departed Assam from Mohanbari Airport in Dibrugarh around noon. Prashantho got us there on time, and we fell into the airport waiting room with an exhaustion that was mental as much as physical.

Our drives the previous two days were long and hard—more than 700 km (nearly 450 miles). To squeeze so many things into each day, Prashantho had driven hard, once reaching 120 km/hr (75mph) on a stretch of good new road in the far east. But most of the kilometers had been pot-hole rutted dodge-'em at 45 mph. We were jounced around and stressed by the need to keep our eyes glued to the road ahead so we could help Prashantho drive.

Still, we were grateful to Prashantho and Sumitra for spending two and a half days hauling us out to the farthest reaches of the nation of India and bringing us back to something approximating civilization. Given the intensity of our experiences, it seemed as if we had known them for years, and we tipped them accordingly.

Then it was onto the plane for a short flight to Kolkata.

In Dad's day, the military ran a daily flight from nearby "Dum Dum" (Doom Dooma) airstrip to Kolkata. It was called "the meat plane" as it brought food and other supplies to upper Assam.

On Dad's last flight out of Assam, he flew to Kolkata, undoubtedly gazing out the window at the receding jungle where he had endured such hardships and danger and contemplating the return to such simple pleasures as hot showers, cold drinks and kissing his girlfriend.

Bo and I had a slightly different view. As our plane lifted up above the city of Dubrugarh, we could see the great Brahmaputra River, four or five miles wide there and ruddy from the iron-rich red soil washing down from Tibet.

This leg lasted about three hours, including a stop in Imphal, site of one of the most important and brutal battles in the Burma Campaign. The Japanese sneaked through the jungle into eastern India and laid siege to British-held Imphal, a months-long engagement that saw combatants at one point lobbing hand grenades at each other from opposite ends of a tennis court. British troops under General William Joseph Slim repelled the Japanese at a crucial point in the campaign.

We had no such problems at Imphal, just a brief layover during which we eagerly discussed our next stop: checking into Kolkata's brand new Hyatt Regency, which I had booked with points.

Bo's daughter Brack says when you are traveling, you spend a lot of time on elemental things like money, tickets, passport—to which I would add "bathrooms." I declined a cold shower at Dihing camp, so I was looking forward to getting to the Hyatt Regency in Kolkata and enjoying a few simple pleasures.

I'm going to take a hot shower and wash my hair!

First, though, we had a most civilized three-hour tour of Kolkata. Since we had only the one night there, I had emailed ahead and asked if we could drive around a bit between airport and hotel, mentioning the burning ghats, Howrah Bridge and the Victoria Palace. The Palace was closed before we got there—sorry to miss that. It's bigger than the Taj Mahal, a museum and monument. We also missed going to the races. Happily, when Katie Bo went to Kolkata in 2018, she had a racing contact (she has racing contacts everywhere in the world) who arranged for her to spend a lovely afternoon in the restricted area of the Royal Calcutta Turf Club. She lives a glamorous life.

Saha Subhashish was our very professional driver who manfully worked through the five o'clock traffic to show us the Howrah Bridge, the old British quarter and the burning ghats along the sacred Ganges River. Dad had stayed nearby in the Grand Hotel, so once again we followed his footsteps.

Saha, tall, erect and proper, drove us around and pointed things out, answering questions as well as possible without overdoing the talking. We did learn that he had gotten married about nine months previously and his wife was expecting a baby in two months. He had not celebrated Holi because he took her to the doctor for a checkup.

Saha was determined to show us Kolkata, despite the horrendous traffic at that hour. Kolkata seems to work, as opposed to Delhi, which is a pathetic wreck of a city. Delhi has that crumbling, decayed look of a Caribbean island (the tropics). There are lovely old buildings, all filthy and unkempt, and it's all overlaid by the air pollution and squatters and animals everyplace.

Whereas Kolkata looks a lot like New York—many fine new buildings, many maintained old buildings. There's a section of old British buildings with trees growing out of the mortar four stories up, untouched as though they are part of a designated heritage area. The slums are there and the squatters along the roads, as in all of India, but in between there are clean well-maintained areas. The roads are good, many of them restricted to cars only—no animals, no trucks, no pedestrians. The garment district and other product market areas all look like New York—crowded and multi-cultural but no animals and no squatters.

The only place we parked and got out was at the burning ghats along the Ganges River. The word "ghat" means steps, and the burning ghats are cremation sites with steps down to the river's edge where the ashes are scattered.

It was hard to get to the ghats, which are in old Kolkata, which is full of narrow winding streets crowded with shops, pedestrians, bikes and traffic. Unlike Delhi, it's actually beautiful in a way. The many old buildings from the Raj are still in use, often covered by the roots of some tree that grows down the walls. The wide use of wrought iron calls to mind the French Quarter in New Orleans.

Saha wound through the streets endlessly—I don't know how he found his way. Eventually we inched alongside the river in a narrow street that didn't seem suited for traffic. There were low buildings on the river side and a concrete wall hemming us in on the other. Squatters were camped along the wall, mothers in bright saris tending a bowl of mess on a small fire as brown babies in filthy underpants played or cried nearby.

On the river side, in front of the buildings were the ubiquitous small merchants of mush or fruit or accessories to cremation. Apparently, yellow is important for the shroud, and small orange carnations are arranged around the body.

Saha had a hard time finding a place to park, needless to say, as squatters, merchants, hangers-on, parked vehicles and traffic clogged the roadway thoroughly. At one point we met an enormous Tata commercial carrier—he liked to never got through and we thought, Why would he even try to bring a truck in here?

You reach the cremation sites through archways that open on to a couple of rooms and have access steps to the river. Some have electric crematories and some have open wood fires.

Bo had second thoughts about intruding on the funerals. I was very interested to see what it looked like, from a reporter's point of view. We asked Saha if it was ok, and he said, "Don't be taking photographs." Since he had worked so hard to get us there and find a parking place, I felt we should get out and walk around.

We stuck out like sore thumbs but we followed Saha, who strode through the street in his white jacket and dark slacks, somehow above the scene. The street seemed to part for him, while Bo and I dodged cars and carts.

At the first ghat, he said he couldn't go in because he had just gotten married—it would be bad luck—but he told us how far we could go. We walked past several bodies of old women laid out on what looked like VMI sleeping racks on the right. A black and white bitch lay nearby while her puppies tussled. There were several oval pits hacked out of the concrete, maybe eighteen inches wide and three feet long, that we assumed were crematory pits. Various lame and afflicted-looking people sat around and smoked or lay on the stone floor. Ahead of us, wide stone steps—the actual ghats—spilled a few feet down a short ramp to the river where a teenaged boy scooped a pile of ashes into the river.

Up some steps to the left was an open-air cremation area, where four fires burned the last remains of somebody. Around the cremation fires on two sides were stone bleachers where the bereaved sat and talked and mourned. No one paid any attention to us.

Farther along the street, we found a building with electric crematories. As soon we passed through a wide opening from the street, we saw on the left a row of half a dozen bodies awaiting cremation. On the right were two round doors that presumably covered the furnace.

We didn't tarry or stare, so it's hard to remember details. In any event, by then we were fading fast and ready for our hotel.

When Saha pulled up in front of the Hyatt Regency, we were agape. After spending the past few nights in a basha with mosquito netting and no power, after hurtling through mudbogs and dodging all grades of traffic, we found ourselves back in civilization. The Hyatt Regency looked like a cross between the Crystal Palace and the Victor Emmanuel Monument in Rome, shiny, multi-layered, modern, palatial. It was so swanky I was afraid they wouldn't let Butch and Sundance come in with so much trail dust on their boots.

But they did. And we gawked at the room like hicks. Well, Bo did. I gawked at the bathroom, where I took a hot shower for an hour!

Then we went to the bar and raised a glass Dad's birthday. And another one to the Ledo Road! And another to Professor Sharma! And another to the pink squeaky toy! And another one to the tiger we didn't see.

Major H. V. Traywick
1918-2006

Epilogue

It was hard to leave India. I had become quite attached to the country and the people and wanted to stay longer. But we had more research to do. Bo and I flew out of Kolkata on March 24, returning to Dubai for a few days of exploring the U.A.E.—also a stop on Dad's world tour in the 1940s. First, we had to retrieve the red bag from storage at the airport—at a price that rivaled the replacement cost of our dress-up clothes contained therein.

We found another fascinating driver to show us around, a man from Pakistan who said he worked seven days a week and went home once a year to see his wife and children. He drove us to Sharja, where Dad's burning airplane landed in January 1945. At the time, Sharja was a sand bar, a fuel dump filled with 55-gallon drums as far as the eye could see, Dad said. Now it is filled with faux-classical architecture reminiscent of the strip in Las Vegas.

At our request, our driver drove us out across the desert to Al Ain where they have a camel market. Bo tried out his Farsi and later found he had bought three camels. Alas, we had no way to get them home. Sort of like the inlaid marble tabletop in Agra.

Katie Bo came with us. She did a double-take when Bo and I looked into a pen full of goats and simultaneously exclaimed, "It's Nanny!" Not grandmother Nana, but a veritable twin of the Toggenburg goat Dad bought when we were children.

Katie Bo took us to a hookah bar, and we tried smoking various flavors of substances that may or may not have been legal. We also went to an allegedly traditional souk, or market, which had been cleaned up for tourists. Bo tried on turbans, and I bought an elephant.

We visited a mall with an indoor ski slope that was not as big as Whistler Mountain but probably competitive with the Homestead. This was not one of Dad's stops on the way home, but we felt obliged to look at it anyway.

Our visit culminated with a fabulous night at the Dubai World Cup. We did Virginia proud in our dress-up clothes plucked from the red bag, putting on a classy sartorial look for the extravagant event being held for the first time at the rebuilt Medan Race Course. Apparently, the previous iteration wasn't

elaborate enough, so Sheikh Mohammed tore it down and built an entirely new palace for horse racing in the desert. We were suitably impressed. The races were exciting but somewhat upstaged by the fireworks and special effects, which rivaled any live performance by a country music singer on tour.

At last, our brain cells having been electrified by two weeks of cultural shock and awe, we headed home. While it took Dad three weeks and fourteen different flights to get from Ledo to Ft. Dix, N.J.—including one plane that caught on fire—we kicked back on an Emirates jet that zipped us home in eleven hours, where we learned that India won the Cricket World Cup by six wickets!

India is a country in transit – and transition. All around are the decaying remnants of the Raj: elegant British architecture with trees growing out of the mortar, all atop the crumbling remains of seven civilizations that existed there prior. India is old. Old but not tired, as the country seethes with energy. The roads are jam packed with people scurrying to and fro, four to a motor scooter. Out of the dust of centuries here and there arise gleaming shrines and five-star hotels. Since Dad was there and since India demanded its independence in '47, perhaps a third of the populace has clawed its way out of poverty into the middle class. Of course, in a country of 1,300 million people, that still leaves a lot of people scrounging through garbage heaps or selling dried cow dung for a few rupees a day. Yet cell phones and motorbikes are ubiquitous, perhaps defining modern India.

We were fascinated to see India in all her contradictions as she struggles to reconcile centuries-old traditions and competing cultures with twenty-first century technology and customs. As I write this in 2023, India has just landed a space vehicle on the Moon, and India has some of the top people in science and industry in the world, yet it is still a country where boys ride elephants down the road and women collect cow dung for fuel. Overall, we found the people to be enterprising, cheerful and welcoming, and we felt privileged to visit their home.

Bo and I had a grand time together, irrespective of the research aspect of the trip. Once back home and back at work on my bio-memoir of my parents' exotic World War II romance, I found the trip had enriched my writing immeasurably. Even though I had been limited to a brief, distant view of the Burmese border, my experiences in India had given me a strong feel for the physical and cultural environment Dad lived in during 1943-1944. I saw the cities, the mixture of ancient and modern, the hordes of humanity. I saw the land, the tangle of jungle growth, the rhinos and rainbow of birds. I ate the food, talked with the people, admired the beauty and deplored the filth. And I felt the energy of more than a billion people walking driving running towards a future of upward mobility.

My book about Mom and Dad in World War II, ***The Last Romantic War***, has been in print for almost three years, and the reception has been gratifying. Everyone from serious historians to teachers to casual readers has raved about feeling as though they experienced the events, places and moods I described.

Thank you, Dean King.

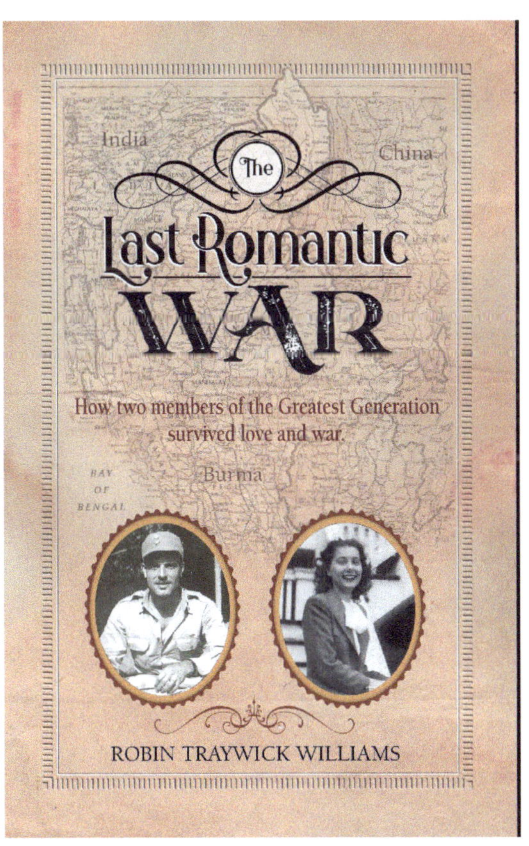

THE STORY THAT STARTED IT ALL —

ACKNOWLEDGEMENTS

Dean King made me go, but Bo Traywick made sure I got there and back safely. I'm indebted to them both.

Cricket cheered me on, as always. Thanks, sweetheart.

Most of the people who made the trip to India possible are acknowledged throughout the text: our drivers and guides, the folks at IndiaMike.com and AmazingArunachelPradesh.com, as well as the authority on the Stilwell Road, Professor Hitendra Nath Sharma. I'm grateful for their time and graciousness.

My friend and colleague from the *Richmond Times-Dispatch*, Paula Squires, gave the manuscript a thorough read and provided excellent advice and welcome encouragement for completing the project. I'm deeply appreciative.

I'm always touched by the personal care and professional talent that Wayne and Dianne Dementi put into all my books, including this one.

Jayne Hushen wowed me again with a beautiful and compelling book cover.

And many thanks to Al Gore for inventing the internet, without which I could not have found all the wonderful Indian people who showed us around.

ABOUT THE AUTHOR

Robin Traywick Williams is an award-winning journalist, author, storyteller and horsewoman.

During her eclectic career, Robin has served as a feature writer for the *Richmond Times-Dispatch,* chairman of the Virginia Racing Commission, president of the Thoroughbred Retirement Foundation and cchief of staff for the lieutenant governor of Virginia. She has also served on the board of a publicly-held bank.

She holds a master's degree from Hollins University and is the author of five books. She and her husband live in central Virginia.